The AI Cure: Innovations In Healthcare Business

Srikanth Suryadevara

Table of Contents

Author Bio

Srikanth Suryadevara is a highly experienced Senior .NET Developer and Technical Lead with over 12 years of expertise in designing, developing, and maintaining robust applications and systems. Proficient in a wide range of .NET frameworks, C#, ASP.NET, angular and related Microsoft technologies, Srikanth Suryadevara has a proven track record of leading technical teams, architecting solutions, and driving innovation in complex software projects. With a deep understanding of software development life cycles, he excels in delivering scalable, high-performance solutions that meet both technical and business requirements.

Reviewers

Anil Kumar Yadav Yanamala achieved in the field of AI and data protection is a significant milestone, often marked by contributions to improving privacy, security, and ethical standards in the ever-evolving digital landscape. It involves the development of innovative solutions that safeguard personal data while balancing the need for technological advancement. Achieved in AI and data protection within government institutions which are crucial for ensuring the privacy and security of citizens' data while implementing advanced technologies. Governments worldwide are increasingly adopting AI to improve public services, cybersecurity, and data management. However, with this adoption comes the responsibility to protect sensitive information and uphold ethical standards.

Chapter 1: The Evolution of AI in Business Decision Making

Chapter 1: The Evolution of AI in Business Decision Making

Chapter 1 sets the stage by exploring the journey of Artificial Intelligence (AI) from its conceptual beginnings to its present-day role as a key driver of business decision making. This chapter provides a comprehensive look at how AI has evolved over the decades, transitioning from a theoretical concept into a practical tool that revolutionizes the way businesses operate and make decisions. The chapter begins by tracing the **historical context of AI** in business, starting from the early days of AI research in the 1950s. Initially, AI was seen as a futuristic technology with limited real-world application, but it has gradually matured with advancements in computing power, algorithms, and data availability. The chapter highlights key milestones in AI's development, such as the advent of machine learning in the 1980s and the rapid growth of data analytics in the early 2000s, which set the stage for AI's current influence in decision-making processes. Next, the chapter delves into the **rise of data-driven decision making**, a significant shift in business operations that began with the digital revolution. As companies began to amass vast amounts of data, the need for more sophisticated tools to analyze and make sense of this data grew. AI emerged as the perfect solution, enabling businesses to automate decision-making processes and uncover insights that would have been impossible to detect manually. This section explains how AI-driven analytics, predictive models, and machine learning algorithms transformed data into a powerful strategic asset. The chapter also examines the **current role of AI in business decision making**, detailing how AI is being used today to enhance decision accuracy and speed. Businesses now use AI to analyze customer behavior, forecast market trends, optimize supply chains, and improve operational efficiency. Real-world examples showcase how companies like Amazon, Google, and Netflix are leveraging AI to stay ahead of their competition by making smarter, faster decisions. As AI continues to evolve, the chapter concludes by discussing the **future of AI in business strategy**.

Introduction

This section explores emerging AI technologies, such as deep learning, natural language processing (NLP), and AI-driven automation, which promise to further revolutionize decision making. It also touches on the potential challenges, such as ethical considerations, data privacy concerns, and the need for regulatory oversight, that businesses will need to navigate as AI becomes even more integral to their operations.

1.1 The Historical Context of AI in Business

The journey of artificial intelligence (AI) in business decision making traces back to the mid-20th century when the first digital computers emerged. Early AI concepts were rooted in attempts to mimic human reasoning and problem-solving capabilities. During the 1950s and 1960s, AI pioneers like Alan Turing and John McCarthy laid the groundwork for the development of intelligent machines. However, these early efforts were limited by computational power and the lack of sophisticated algorithms. By the 1980s, expert systems gained traction in business applications. These rule-based systems could simulate human decision-making by encoding expert knowledge into a structured format. While limited to specific domains, expert systems showed the potential of AI in solving complex problems, particularly in industries like healthcare, finance, and manufacturing. However, these systems required significant human input and lacked the ability to learn from data, which hampered their scalability. The next major leap occurred in the late 1990s and early 2000s with the advent of machine learning (ML), a subfield of AI that enabled systems to learn from data and improve over time without explicit programming. ML algorithms began to make headway in business settings, from customer segmentation to fraud detection, as the internet and digital transformation drove an explosion of available data.

1.2 The Rise of Data-Driven Decision Making

With the proliferation of big data in the 21st century, businesses began to recognize the potential of using AI to turn vast amounts of data into valuable insights. This gave rise to data-driven decision making, where organizations rely on data and analytics to guide strategy, operations, and customer interactions.

AI became essential in helping businesses process and analyze massive datasets that were too complex for human interpretation. Companies like Google, Amazon, and Netflix pioneered the use of AI to optimize search algorithms, recommend products, and personalize user experiences. AI-powered tools allowed businesses to identify patterns, predict outcomes, and make more informed decisions, thereby increasing efficiency and competitiveness.

The shift toward data-driven decision making was further accelerated by advancements in cloud computing and storage, which made it easier and cheaper for businesses to access and process data at scale. AI became a vital component in transforming raw data into actionable business intelligence.

1.3 Understanding AI Technologies and Their Business Applications

AI encompasses a wide range of technologies, each with its specific applications in business decision making. The most important AI technologies include:

- **Machine Learning (ML):** ML algorithms enable systems to learn from historical data and predict future outcomes. In business, ML is used for demand forecasting, fraud detection, recommendation systems, and customer segmentation. Companies leverage ML to make decisions faster and more accurately, automating processes that once required manual intervention.

- **Natural Language Processing (NLP):** NLP allows machines to understand and process human language. Businesses use NLP for customer support (e.g., chatbots), sentiment analysis, and text mining. It enhances communication with customers and extracts insights from unstructured data like social media posts and emails.

- **Robotic Process Automation (RPA):** RPA automates repetitive, rule-based tasks, such as data entry and invoice processing. This frees up human workers to focus on higher-level decision making. RPA, combined with AI, improves operational efficiency and reduces the risk of human error in business processes.

- **Deep Learning (DL):** A subset of ML, deep learning involves neural networks that mimic the human brain's structure and function. It is particularly powerful in applications like image recognition, autonomous vehicles, and voice assistants. Businesses are using DL to enhance product development and customer experiences, such as personalizing content recommendations and improving visual search capabilities.

These AI technologies enable businesses to move beyond simple data analysis to predictive and prescriptive decision making, providing a competitive edge in today's data-driven world.

1.4 Case Studies of Early AI Adopters

Several businesses have been early adopters of AI and have successfully integrated it into their decision-making processes:

- **Netflix:** One of the earliest and most successful adopters of AI, Netflix uses machine learning algorithms to analyze user preferences and viewing habits. This data is used to provide personalized content recommendations, which keeps users engaged and helps the platform retain subscribers. Netflix's AI-powered decision-making system has not only improved user experience but also guided its investment in original content based on predicted viewer demand.

- **Amazon:** AI is central to Amazon's business operations, from optimizing logistics and supply chains to powering Alexa, its virtual assistant. Amazon's recommendation engine, driven by AI, generates personalized product suggestions based on customer browsing and purchasing behavior, significantly boosting sales.

- **Google:** Google has implemented AI in almost every aspect of its operations, particularly in its search engine algorithms. Machine learning models analyze billions of data points to provide users with the most relevant search results. Google's AI also powers its advertising platform, helping businesses target the right customers with precision.

- **JPMorgan Chase:** In the financial sector, JPMorgan Chase has integrated AI into its decision-making process to detect fraud, manage risk, and enhance customer service. AI-driven algorithms analyze transaction patterns in real time, identifying anomalies that could indicate fraudulent activities. AI also aids in improving customer experience by automating routine tasks like loan approvals.

These examples illustrate how AI can drive business innovation, improve customer satisfaction, and enhance operational efficiency.

1.5 The Future of AI in Business Strategy

The future of AI in business decision making is bright, with continued advancements in technology poised to transform industries further. As AI becomes more sophisticated, businesses will be able to automate more complex decisions, leaving human workers to focus on creative and strategic tasks. Some key trends include:

- **AI-Driven Decision Support Systems:** AI systems will increasingly act as decision support tools, providing business leaders with real-time insights and recommendations. These systems will integrate data from various sources, making it easier to navigate complex business environments and make more informed strategic decisions.

- **AI in Autonomous Decision Making:** As AI technologies mature, businesses may begin to trust AI systems to make decisions autonomously. This could range from dynamic pricing models in e-commerce to self-driving supply chains in manufacturing and logistics. Autonomous decision making can reduce response times and optimize efficiency across business operations.

- **Human-AI Collaboration:** The future will likely see increased collaboration between AI systems and human decision makers. AI can process data at an unprecedented scale, while humans bring creativity, intuition, and emotional intelligence. Together, they can form more effective decision-making teams that combine the strengths of both AI and human expertise.

- **Ethical and Regulatory Challenges:** As AI becomes more ingrained in business strategy, ethical and regulatory challenges will become more prominent. Businesses will need to address concerns around data privacy, bias in AI algorithms, and the societal impacts of automation. Governments are also likely to introduce more stringent regulations governing the use of AI in decision making, making it essential for businesses to adopt responsible AI practices.

In summary, AI has evolved from a theoretical concept to a powerful tool that is reshaping how businesses make decisions. Companies that embrace AI will have a significant advantage in navigating the increasingly complex and data-driven business landscape, but they must also be mindful of the ethical and regulatory implications as they integrate AI into their strategies.

1.1 The Historical Context of AI in Business

Artificial Intelligence (AI) has been a concept of fascination since the mid-20th century, long before it became a central player in business decision-making. Its evolution in the business world reflects broader advances in computing, data science, and algorithmic innovation. The integration of AI into business strategies did not occur overnight; it has been a gradual journey influenced by technological advancements, market demands, and the increasing complexity of business environments.

Early Days: The Foundations of AI

The field of AI began in the 1950s when pioneers like Alan Turing and John McCarthy laid the theoretical groundwork. Turing's famous question, "Can machines think?" and his subsequent development of the Turing Test sparked discussions about the potential of intelligent machines. Around the same time, John McCarthy coined the term "artificial intelligence" and organized the Dartmouth Conference in 1956, which is widely regarded as the official birth of AI as a field of study.

In the early days, AI research focused on replicating human cognitive processes, such as reasoning, learning, and problem-solving. However, progress was slow due to the limitations of computational power and the complexity of modeling human intelligence. Early business applications of AI were largely experimental, limited to specific tasks like basic pattern recognition and logic-based problem solving.

The Rise of Expert Systems in the 1980s

By the 1980s, AI research had advanced to the point where businesses began experimenting with **expert systems**— software designed to mimic human experts by applying predefined rules to solve complex problems within a specific domain. These systems could make decisions based on a set of "if-then" rules encoded by experts. Industries such as healthcare, finance, and manufacturing used expert systems for tasks like diagnosing diseases, managing financial portfolios, and optimizing production processes.

For example, **XCON**, an expert system developed by Digital Equipment Corporation (DEC) in the late 1970s, was one of the most famous applications of AI in business at that time. XCON helped DEC configure orders for its computer systems, saving the company millions of dollars in operational costs by reducing configuration errors.

However, expert systems had several limitations. They required extensive manual input from domain experts to define the rules, were inflexible in adapting to new data, and were computationally expensive to scale. Despite these challenges, expert systems laid the groundwork for AI's role in business decision-making.

The Emergence of Machine Learning in the 1990s

In the 1990s, AI took a significant leap forward with the emergence of **machine learning (ML)**, a subset of AI that focused on the development of algorithms capable of learning from data rather than relying on hard-coded rules. This shift was largely driven by the explosion of digital data and advancements in computational power.

Machine learning introduced a new paradigm in business decision-making. Instead of creating complex rule-based systems, businesses could now train algorithms on historical data to identify patterns, make predictions, and automate decisions. Industries like finance and retail were among the first to adopt machine learning for applications such as fraud detection, credit scoring, and customer segmentation.

For instance, **credit card companies** began using machine learning algorithms to detect fraudulent transactions in real time by analyzing transaction patterns. **Retailers** used machine learning to analyze consumer behavior and optimize pricing strategies, inventory management, and marketing campaigns. This shift from rule-based expert systems to data-driven machine learning marked a turning point in AI's impact on business decision-making.

The Era of Big Data and Deep Learning in the 2000s

The 2000s saw the rise of **big data**, which refers to the massive volumes of structured and unstructured data generated by businesses, consumers, and digital platforms. This era was characterized by a growing recognition that data could be a valuable asset for making more informed business decisions. However, the sheer volume and complexity of data required more sophisticated AI tools for analysis and decision-making.

Enter **deep learning**, a branch of machine learning that leverages artificial neural networks to analyze complex datasets, including images, text, and speech. Deep learning models, particularly those based on **convolutional neural networks (CNNs)** and **recurrent neural networks (RNNs)**, enabled businesses to automate more complex tasks, such as image recognition, natural language processing, and autonomous decision-making.

For example, **Google** employed deep learning algorithms to improve the accuracy of its search engine, while **Amazon** used it to enhance product recommendations and personalize the shopping experience. Deep learning's ability to process and learn from vast amounts of unstructured data, such as social media posts, emails, and video content, opened up new possibilities for businesses to gain insights and make strategic decisions.

AI's Integration into Business Strategy in the 2010s

In the 2010s, AI became more deeply integrated into mainstream business strategies. Cloud computing and the availability of affordable computing power further accelerated the adoption of AI. Companies could now harness the capabilities of AI without the need for expensive on-premise infrastructure. AI-driven platforms, such as **Amazon Web Services (AWS)**, **Google Cloud**, and **Microsoft Azure**, provided businesses with the tools and frameworks needed to implement AI at scale.

During this period, businesses across various sectors adopted AI for a wide range of applications, including:

- **Customer personalization** (e.g., recommendation engines, targeted advertising)
- **Operational optimization** (e.g., supply chain management, predictive maintenance)
- **Financial forecasting** (e.g., stock market prediction, risk management)
- **Human resource management** (e.g., AI-driven recruitment, employee retention analytics)

Industries such as **healthcare**, **automotive**, and **retail** saw transformative changes as AI-driven automation and analytics became central to decision-making processes. For instance, **Tesla** employed AI in developing autonomous vehicles, while **Walmart** used AI to optimize supply chain operations and improve customer service through chatbots.

The Present and Future of AI in Business Decision Making

As we enter the 2020s, AI continues to evolve, becoming a crucial element of business decision-making at all levels—from operational efficiency to strategic planning. Businesses are now using AI to make real-time decisions, from dynamic pricing models in e-commerce to personalized marketing campaigns in consumer goods.

The future of AI in business will likely involve greater **automation, personalization**, and **predictive capabilities**. AI systems are expected to become more autonomous, capable of making complex decisions without human intervention, and businesses will increasingly rely on AI to navigate uncertainty and market volatility. In summary, AI's historical trajectory in business decision-making has been a journey from theoretical concepts to practical applications that enhance efficiency, drive innovation, and transform industries. As AI continues to advance, its role in shaping business strategy will only grow, making it an indispensable tool for organizations looking to stay competitive in the digital age.

1.2 The Rise of Data-Driven Decision Making

The evolution of business decision-making has been shaped by the increasing availability of data and the development of technologies capable of processing and analyzing that data. Traditionally, business leaders relied on intuition, experience, and limited data sets when making decisions. However, the rise of digital technologies and the explosive growth of data in the early 21st century brought about a fundamental shift toward data-driven decision making (DDDM). This shift has been accelerated by advancements in artificial intelligence (AI) and machine learning (ML), which allow businesses to extract actionable insights from vast amounts of data.

The Data Explosion: Foundations of Data-Driven Decision Making

The digital transformation that began in the late 1990s and early 2000s brought with it unprecedented levels of data generation. Businesses began to realize that data wasn't just a byproduct of their operations but a valuable asset that could inform strategy, improve efficiency, and enhance customer experiences. The growth of e-commerce, social media, and connected devices (Internet of Things, IoT) led to the creation of massive amounts of data related to consumer behavior, operational performance, and market trends.

Big data refers to these massive datasets that are too large, complex, or varied for traditional data processing tools to handle. Businesses found themselves grappling with the **three Vs** of big data: volume, velocity, and variety:

- **Volume** refers to the sheer amount of data generated by businesses, customers, and machines.
- **Velocity** relates to the speed at which data is generated and must be processed.
- **Variety** refers to the different forms of data, including structured (e.g., databases), semi-structured (e.g., XML files), and unstructured (e.g., videos, social media posts).

As organizations struggled to manage these vast datasets, they recognized the need for advanced technologies to help make sense of the information and transform it into actionable insights.

AI and Machine Learning: Enabling Data-Driven Insights

The rise of data-driven decision making is closely tied to the development of AI, particularly **machine learning (ML)**, which allowed businesses to automate the process of analyzing large datasets and uncovering patterns. Machine learning algorithms, which can learn from historical data, enabled businesses to go beyond descriptive analytics (what happened) and embrace predictive analytics (what will happen) and prescriptive analytics (what should be done).

AI-powered tools allowed businesses to:

- **Predict customer behavior:** Machine learning models could analyze customer data to forecast purchasing decisions, enabling personalized marketing and product recommendations.
- **Optimize operations:** AI could analyze data from supply chains, production lines, and logistics networks to identify inefficiencies and recommend process improvements.
- **Detect anomalies and risks:** AI systems, particularly in finance and cybersecurity, could detect fraudulent transactions, identify potential security breaches, and assess operational risks based on historical patterns.

For example, **Google** used AI and machine learning to optimize its ad targeting algorithms, analyzing vast amounts of data from search queries, browsing behavior, and demographics to deliver personalized ads in real time. **Amazon** used AI to power its recommendation engine, analyzing customer data to suggest products that increased engagement and sales.

The Shift from Gut Instinct to Data-Driven Decisions

Before the rise of data-driven decision making, many business decisions were based on **gut instinct** or **experience**. Executives and managers often made strategic choices based on their intuition or limited sets of historical data. While this approach sometimes led to success, it was inherently risky, as it relied on subjective judgment and potentially incomplete information.

With the rise of big data and AI, businesses recognized that they could reduce uncertainty and improve decision accuracy by using data to guide their choices. **Data-driven decision making (DDDM)** involves using data analysis and AI-powered insights to inform every aspect of business operations, from product development and marketing to customer service and financial planning.

This approach brought several advantages:

- **Improved accuracy:** Decisions based on data are typically more accurate and reliable than those based on intuition, as they are grounded in evidence.
- **Faster decision-making:** AI can process and analyze data far more quickly than humans, allowing businesses to make decisions in real time.
- **Scalability:** Data-driven decision-making frameworks can scale across different departments, regions, and business units, allowing organizations to apply insights broadly.
- **Continuous improvement:** AI systems can learn and improve over time, refining their predictions and recommendations as they are exposed to more data.

This shift toward DDDM fundamentally changed the culture of decision making in business. It required organizations to invest in new technologies, create data-driven teams, and develop a mindset that values objective, evidence-based approaches to decision making.

Real-World Applications of Data-Driven Decision Making

Data-driven decision making has become a critical tool for companies in various industries. Several leading organizations have embraced DDDM to gain a competitive edge, optimize their operations, and improve customer satisfaction.

- **E-commerce:** Companies like **Amazon** and **Alibaba** use data-driven decision making to power recommendation engines, forecast demand, and optimize pricing strategies. By analyzing user data such as purchase history, browsing behavior, and reviews, these companies create personalized experiences that keep customers engaged and loyal.

- **Finance:** Financial institutions like **JPMorgan Chase** and **Goldman Sachs** rely on AI and data-driven models to assess risk, detect fraud, and inform investment strategies. AI-driven models analyze market data, customer behavior, and macroeconomic trends to make real-time decisions that minimize risk and maximize profitability.

- **Healthcare:** Healthcare providers are using AI to analyze patient data and improve clinical decision-making. Data-driven models can predict patient outcomes, identify high-risk individuals, and recommend personalized treatment plans. For instance, **IBM Watson Health** has developed AI systems that analyze medical records, research papers, and clinical trial data to assist doctors in diagnosing and treating diseases like cancer.

- **Manufacturing:** In manufacturing, companies like **General Electric (GE)** and **Siemens** use AI to predict equipment failures, optimize maintenance schedules, and improve product quality. By analyzing sensor data from machines and production lines, these companies can make proactive decisions that reduce downtime and increase operational efficiency.

Challenges in Implementing Data-Driven Decision Making

While the benefits of data-driven decision making are clear, implementing this approach comes with its own set of challenges. Businesses must address several key issues to fully realize the potential of DDDM:

- **Data quality and governance:** Businesses need to ensure that the data they collect is accurate, complete, and relevant. Poor data quality can lead to incorrect insights and flawed decision making.

Establishing robust data governance frameworks is essential to maintaining data integrity.

- **Data privacy and security:** As businesses collect more data on customers, operations, and markets, they must ensure that this data is protected from breaches and misuse. Data privacy regulations, such as GDPR in Europe and CCPA in California, place strict requirements on how businesses collect, store, and use personal data.

- **Cultural shift:** Transitioning to a data-driven culture requires a fundamental shift in how decisions are made across the organization. Employees must be trained to trust data-driven insights and use them to inform their decision-making processes. This can be particularly challenging for organizations that have historically relied on experience and intuition.

- **AI bias:** AI models are only as good as the data they are trained on. If historical data contains biases, AI systems may perpetuate or even amplify those biases in their predictions and recommendations. Businesses must take steps to ensure that their data and AI models are fair and unbiased.

The Future of Data-Driven Decision Making

As businesses continue to generate and collect ever-larger datasets, the future of data-driven decision making looks promising. Emerging technologies such as **edge computing**, **quantum computing**, and **5G** will further enhance the ability of organizations to analyze data and make real-time decisions.

Additionally, advancements in **explainable AI** (XAI) will help address concerns about transparency and accountability in AI-driven decision making. XAI aims to make AI models more interpretable, allowing business leaders to understand the reasoning behind AI-generated insights and recommendations.

In the coming years, businesses that embrace data-driven decision making will have a significant competitive advantage, as they will be able to make faster, more accurate, and more informed decisions. The integration of AI and big data analytics into every aspect of business strategy will become the norm, reshaping industries and redefining how businesses operate in the digital age.

The rise of data-driven decision making marks one of the most transformative shifts in business strategy over the last few decades. Historically, business leaders relied heavily on intuition, past experiences, and limited datasets to make crucial decisions. The advent of digital technologies, coupled with the explosion of data generated by the internet, social media, and connected devices, has dramatically altered this approach. The 21st century introduced a new era where decisions are increasingly grounded in empirical data, allowing businesses to uncover patterns, predict trends, and optimize operations with unprecedented accuracy. This shift not only changed how companies operate but also how they compete, with those embracing data-driven strategies gaining a significant edge over competitors still dependent on traditional methods.

The foundation of data-driven decision making lies in the concept of **big data**, which refers to the massive amounts of data being generated at an accelerated pace. This data, collected from a variety of sources such as customer interactions, social media, IoT devices, and transactional systems, is often too large and complex for traditional processing tools. The sheer scale of the data available to businesses today creates both opportunities and challenges. On one hand, companies can mine this data to gain valuable insights into customer behavior, market trends, and operational inefficiencies. On the other hand, the sheer volume of information requires advanced analytical tools and AI systems capable of processing and interpreting it in real time. Thus, the rise of data-driven decision making has gone hand in hand with the development of AI technologies, particularly machine learning, which allow businesses to sift through vast datasets and derive actionable insights.

AI has become a cornerstone of data-driven decision making by automating data analysis and providing predictive and prescriptive insights. Traditional data analysis techniques were limited in scope, often only capable of analyzing historical data and providing descriptive insights (i.e., what happened). With AI, businesses can now leverage **predictive analytics** to forecast future trends and outcomes and **prescriptive analytics** to recommend the best course of action based on data-driven insights. For example, machine learning algorithms can analyze vast amounts of consumer data to predict future buying behaviors, enabling companies to personalize marketing campaigns and optimize their product offerings. AI-powered systems can also process data from supply chains, sales channels, and production facilities to identify inefficiencies, predict potential disruptions, and suggest improvements. In doing so, AI not only enhances the decision-making process but also enables businesses to make these decisions faster and with more accuracy.

This shift to data-driven decision making has also radically transformed the role of leadership within organizations. In the past, many business decisions were made based on the intuition and experience of senior executives. While these decision-makers often had years of experience and industry knowledge, their decisions were still subject to human biases and limited data inputs. Today, business leaders are increasingly expected to base their decisions on data-driven insights, requiring a new set of skills and a willingness to trust advanced analytical tools over gut instincts. This has led to the rise of **data-driven cultures** within organizations, where decision-making at all levels is informed by data analysis and AI-powered tools. Companies that successfully cultivate a data-driven culture often see significant benefits, including increased operational efficiency, improved customer satisfaction, and more effective risk management.

Real-world applications of data-driven decision making are widespread across industries. In the financial sector, for instance, banks and investment firms use AI to assess risks, detect fraudulent activities, and automate trading decisions based on market data. Similarly, in retail, companies like **Amazon** and **Walmart** have revolutionized the shopping experience by using data to personalize recommendations, optimize pricing, and manage inventory. Data-driven decision making is also making waves in healthcare, where hospitals and pharmaceutical companies use AI to analyze patient data, predict disease outbreaks, and develop personalized treatment plans. In the manufacturing industry, companies rely on AI to predict machine failures, optimize production schedules, and reduce downtime. Across all these industries, the common thread is the reliance on data and AI to inform and improve business strategies.

Despite its clear benefits, the implementation of data-driven decision making comes with challenges. One of the most significant hurdles is ensuring data quality. Inaccurate, incomplete, or outdated data can lead to flawed insights and poor decisions. Therefore, businesses must invest in robust data governance frameworks to ensure that their data is reliable and up to date. Another challenge is the **privacy**

and security of data. As companies collect more information on their customers and operations, they face increasing scrutiny over how this data is stored, shared, and used. Laws such as the **General Data Protection Regulation (GDPR)** in the European Union and the **California Consumer Privacy Act (CCPA)** in the United States impose strict regulations on how businesses handle personal data. Companies must navigate these legal requirements while ensuring that they can still leverage data to drive decision-making.

Moreover, transitioning to a data-driven culture often requires a significant **organizational shift**. Employees, particularly those in leadership positions, must be trained to trust data over intuition and to use AI tools to inform their decisions. This shift can be particularly difficult in industries that have traditionally relied on experience-based decision making. Companies must also address the issue of **AI bias**. Since AI systems learn from historical data, they can sometimes perpetuate the biases present in that data, leading to unfair or discriminatory outcomes. For example, an AI system used in hiring might unintentionally favor certain demographics if the training data reflects historical biases. To prevent this, businesses must take steps to ensure that their AI models are trained on diverse, representative data and that any potential biases are identified and addressed.

Looking ahead, the future of data-driven decision making is closely tied to ongoing advancements in AI and analytics technologies. Emerging technologies such as **quantum computing**, **edge computing**, and **5G** will further enhance the ability of businesses to process and analyze data in real time, opening up new possibilities for decision-making at scale. Additionally, the development of **explainable AI (XAI)**, which aims to make AI models more transparent and interpretable, will help address concerns about the "black box" nature of AI systems. As businesses continue to generate more data and as AI technology becomes more sophisticated, data-driven decision making will likely become the standard across industries, reshaping how businesses operate and compete in the digital age. In this future, companies that are able to harness the full potential of data and AI will be the ones that thrive.

1.5 The Future of AI in Business Strategy

The future of AI in business strategy is poised to redefine industries, revolutionize decision-making processes, and create unprecedented opportunities for growth and innovation. As artificial intelligence continues to evolve, its role in shaping business strategies will deepen, becoming integral to how companies operate, compete, and create value. The rapid advancements in AI, machine learning, natural language processing, and data analytics will enable businesses to not only automate routine tasks but also develop highly sophisticated strategies that are data-driven, agile, and adaptive to ever-changing market conditions.

One of the most significant ways AI will impact future business strategy is by enabling real-time decision-making on an unparalleled scale. With the advent of **edge computing** and **5G networks**, businesses will be able to process and analyze vast amounts of data instantly, allowing for quicker responses to market changes, consumer behaviors, and operational challenges. AI systems will be capable of identifying trends, predicting outcomes, and recommending strategies with precision, all in real time. This real-time decision-making capability will give businesses a critical competitive advantage, as they can pivot and adapt faster than ever before, capitalizing on emerging opportunities and mitigating risks as they arise.

The rise of **autonomous decision-making systems** will also be a game changer. While AI has already proven its ability to assist humans in decision-making, the future will see AI systems taking on more autonomous roles in formulating and executing business strategies. In areas such as supply chain management, financial trading, and customer service, AI-powered systems will be able to autonomously optimize operations, negotiate deals, and manage customer interactions with minimal human intervention. For instance, AI could autonomously manage an entire supply chain, from procuring raw materials to predicting demand and adjusting production schedules in real time. Similarly, in financial markets, autonomous AI trading systems will make split-second decisions based on complex market data, capitalizing on market inefficiencies far beyond human capabilities.

AI's ability to personalize experiences at scale will further transform business strategies, particularly in customer engagement and marketing. The concept of **hyper-personalization**, driven by AI, will allow businesses to tailor products, services, and marketing messages to individual customer preferences with incredible accuracy. By analyzing vast datasets from customer interactions, purchase histories, and social media activity, AI will enable businesses to deliver highly relevant content and offers to consumers. In retail, for instance, AI-driven personalization engines will recommend products tailored to individual preferences, while in entertainment, AI will curate content for users based on their specific viewing or listening habits. This level of personalization will enhance customer loyalty, drive higher conversion rates, and ultimately lead to increased revenue.

Moreover, the future of AI in business strategy will be characterized by **predictive and prescriptive analytics**. Businesses will increasingly rely on AI to forecast future trends, consumer demands, and market disruptions, allowing them to anticipate changes and plan proactively. Predictive analytics will give companies the foresight to develop strategies that not only react to market conditions but preempt them. For example, AI could analyze economic indicators, consumer sentiment, and historical data to predict market downturns or upswings, enabling companies to adjust their production, marketing, or investment strategies accordingly. Prescriptive analytics will take this a step further by offering actionable recommendations, guiding businesses on the best possible course of action to achieve their goals.

Another major trend will be the growing importance of **AI-driven innovation**. As AI systems become more sophisticated, they will play a pivotal role in ideating and driving innovation across industries. AI will help businesses design new products, optimize existing ones, and discover entirely new business models. In sectors such as healthcare, pharmaceuticals, and manufacturing, AI will accelerate research and development, reducing time-to-market for new drugs, treatments, and technologies. AI systems will also generate insights from complex scientific data, identifying patterns and correlations that were previously undetectable, leading to groundbreaking discoveries and innovations. This will allow businesses to continuously innovate, stay ahead of the competition, and drive growth in increasingly crowded markets.

However, as AI becomes more embedded in business strategy, companies will need to navigate several key challenges. One of the most pressing concerns is the issue of **AI transparency and ethics**. As AI systems take on more decision-making responsibilities, ensuring that these decisions are transparent, explainable, and free from bias will be critical. The rise of **explainable AI (XAI)** will be essential in addressing this challenge. XAI aims to make AI decisions more interpretable by providing clear insights into how algorithms arrive at their conclusions. This transparency will be crucial for gaining the trust of stakeholders, including customers, employees, and regulators, and for ensuring that AI systems are aligned with ethical and legal standards.

Data privacy and security will also remain at the forefront of AI adoption. As businesses increasingly rely on vast amounts of personal and sensitive data to drive AI systems, they must ensure that this data is protected against breaches, misuse, and unauthorized access. Stricter regulations, such as **GDPR** and **CCPA**, are already in place to protect consumer privacy, and businesses will need to continuously adapt their data practices to comply with evolving legal requirements. Companies that fail to safeguard data effectively risk significant reputational and financial damage.

The future of AI in business strategy will also depend on the ability of organizations to develop a **skilled workforce** that can harness the full potential of AI. While AI will automate many tasks, human oversight and expertise will remain essential in interpreting AI-driven insights and making strategic decisions. Businesses will need to invest in training and upskilling employees, ensuring that they have the technical knowledge to work alongside AI systems and the critical thinking skills to make informed decisions based on AI-driven recommendations. The rise of **AI-human collaboration** will create new roles and opportunities, where humans and AI work together to drive business outcomes, combining the strengths of both human intuition and AI's analytical capabilities.

In conclusion, the future of AI in business strategy is one of immense potential and opportunity. AI will enable businesses to operate more efficiently, make better decisions, and innovate faster than ever before. From real-time decision-making and autonomous systems to hyper-personalization and predictive analytics, AI will become a fundamental part of how companies strategize and compete in the marketplace. However, as AI's influence grows, businesses will also need to address challenges related to transparency, ethics, and data privacy, ensuring that their AI-driven strategies are responsible and sustainable. Those organizations that can successfully integrate AI into their strategic frameworks will be well-positioned to thrive in the rapidly evolving digital economy.

Chapter 2: Data as the New Currency: Leveraging AI for Insights

- 2.1 AI's Role in Data Collection and Processing
- 2.2 Data Analytics and Predictive Modeling
- 2.3 Enhancing Business Intelligence through AI
- 2.4 Turning Big Data into Actionable Insights

- 2.5 Overcoming Data Challenges: Privacy, Security, and Bias

Chapter 2: Data as the New Currency: Leveraging AI for Insights

Chapter 2: Data as the New Currency: Leveraging AI for Insights

Chapter 2 explores the concept of data as the driving force behind modern business strategies, emphasizing how AI can be harnessed to extract valuable insights from vast amounts of data. As businesses increasingly rely on data for decision-making, AI becomes a critical tool in transforming raw information into actionable intelligence. This chapter will represent the role of data in today's digital economy and how AI technologies enable organizations to unlock its potential for growth, innovation, and competitiveness.

2.1 AI's Role in Data Collection and Processing

This section examines how AI automates and optimizes the process of gathering, organizing, and processing large volumes of data. AI-powered tools can collect data from multiple sources, such as customer interactions, social media, and IoT devices, and then categorize and process it for analysis. The integration of AI ensures that data is processed faster and more accurately, enabling businesses to stay ahead in competitive industries.

2.2 Data Analytics and Predictive Modeling

Data analytics and predictive modeling are at the core of AI-driven insights. This section discusses how AI uses historical data to build predictive models that can forecast future trends, customer behavior, and market shifts. AI enhances the ability to analyze patterns and correlations within the data, allowing businesses to make proactive decisions, mitigate risks, and optimize operations.

2.3 Enhancing Business Intelligence through AI

AI revolutionizes traditional business intelligence by offering advanced capabilities such as natural language processing (NLP) and machine learning algorithms. This section highlights how AI-driven business intelligence tools improve decision-making processes, enabling organizations to gain deeper insights into customer preferences, market dynamics, and operational performance, leading to smarter and more informed strategic decisions.

2.4 Turning Big Data into Actionable Insights

This section focuses on the challenge of converting vast amounts of unstructured data into actionable insights. AI technologies, such as deep learning and data mining, are crucial in identifying meaningful patterns within large datasets. By analyzing real-time data, AI provides actionable recommendations that can lead to improved customer experiences, product innovations, and market strategies.

2.5 Overcoming Data Challenges: Privacy, Security, and Bias

With the increasing reliance on data, challenges related to privacy, security, and bias have also emerged. This section addresses these critical issues and explores how AI can be used to navigate data protection regulations, ensure security, and mitigate bias in data analysis. AI tools are essential for automating compliance checks, improving data security measures, and ensuring ethical data usage in decision-making.

Introduction

In today's hyper-connected and digital world, data has become the lifeblood of modern businesses, often referred to as the "new currency" driving competitive advantage and innovation. Data is not only a resource but a strategic asset that companies across industries are leveraging to unlock insights, improve operations, and gain a deeper understanding of their customers and markets. The convergence of artificial intelligence (AI) and big data has transformed how businesses harness the power of information, turning vast datasets into actionable insights that fuel decision-making, innovation, and growth. This chapter explores the value of data in the digital economy, how AI enhances data-driven insights, and the strategic advantages businesses can gain by embracing data as their most valuable asset.

2.1 The Data Explosion: A New Age of Information

The modern era has witnessed an unprecedented explosion of data, with more information generated in the last few years than in all of previous human history combined. This surge in data creation has been driven by advances in digital technologies, the proliferation of internet-connected devices, and the rise of social media, e-commerce, and cloud computing. **Big data**, a term used to describe this massive influx of structured and unstructured data, is now seen as one of the most valuable commodities for businesses, governments, and organizations. Every interaction, transaction, and digital footprint creates new data points, providing a treasure trove of information that, if analyzed effectively, can yield profound insights into human behavior, market trends, and operational efficiency.

However, this massive influx of data also presents challenges. The sheer volume, variety, and velocity of data make it difficult for traditional analytics methods to process and analyze it effectively. This is where AI comes into play. AI systems, particularly machine learning and deep learning algorithms, are uniquely equipped to handle the complexity and scale of big data. They can sift through enormous datasets, identify patterns, uncover correlations, and generate insights far beyond human capability. This ability to extract value from data in real time has made AI an essential tool for businesses looking to capitalize on the data explosion.

2.2 The Role of AI in Unlocking Data-Driven Insights

Artificial intelligence has revolutionized how businesses approach data analysis. Traditional data analytics relied on predefined rules and models, which were limited in their ability to adapt to new, complex data. In contrast, AI, especially machine learning algorithms, can learn from data and improve over time, offering businesses a dynamic and flexible approach to data-driven decision-making. AI models can process vast amounts of data from various sources, identify patterns that would be impossible for humans to detect, and make predictions that guide business strategy.

One of the key advantages of AI in data analysis is its ability to handle **unstructured data**. In the past, businesses mostly focused on structured data such as sales numbers, financial reports, and customer databases. However, the majority of data generated today is unstructured, coming from sources like social media posts, emails, images, and video content. AI technologies, such as natural language processing (NLP) and computer vision, allow businesses to analyze this unstructured data, transforming it into valuable insights. For example, NLP can be used to analyze customer reviews, social media comments, and survey responses to gauge sentiment and identify emerging trends, while computer vision can analyze visual data to automate quality control processes in manufacturing.

Another critical area where AI enhances data analysis is in **predictive and prescriptive analytics**. Predictive analytics uses historical data to forecast future trends, while prescriptive analytics goes a step further, offering recommendations on the best course of action based on data-driven insights. AI-powered predictive models can help businesses anticipate customer behavior, market shifts, and operational risks, allowing them to make proactive decisions. For example, retailers can use AI to predict which products are likely to be in high demand during specific times of the year, enabling them to optimize inventory and reduce waste. In the healthcare industry, AI can analyze patient data to predict disease outbreaks or identify individuals at risk of chronic conditions, enabling early intervention and better patient outcomes.

2.3 Data Monetization: Turning Insights into Profit

As data has become more valuable, businesses are increasingly exploring ways to monetize the insights they gain from it. **Data monetization** refers to the process of generating revenue from data by either using it to improve internal operations or selling it to external parties. AI plays a critical role in this process by helping businesses extract and analyze data more effectively, turning raw information into actionable insights that can drive profit.

One way companies monetize data is through **personalization**. By analyzing customer data, businesses can tailor their products, services, and marketing efforts to individual preferences, enhancing the customer experience and increasing sales. Companies like **Netflix** and **Spotify**, for example, use AI-driven recommendation engines to personalize content for their users, keeping them engaged and driving customer loyalty. Similarly, e-commerce giants like **Amazon** analyze purchasing data to suggest products that customers are likely to buy, significantly boosting conversion rates.

Another avenue for data monetization is through **data partnerships**. Businesses can share or sell anonymized datasets to other companies, creating new revenue streams. For example, telecommunications companies may sell location data to retailers, enabling them to better understand customer foot traffic patterns and optimize store locations. However, it's crucial for businesses to ensure that they are complying with privacy regulations, such as **GDPR** and **CCPA**, when engaging in data monetization practices. AI systems can assist with this by automating data anonymization and ensuring that customer information is handled securely and ethically.

Moreover, AI enables **operational optimization**, which indirectly drives profit by improving efficiency and reducing costs. For example, AI can analyze sensor data from manufacturing equipment to predict when machines are likely to fail, enabling companies to perform preventive maintenance and reduce downtime. In logistics, AI can optimize delivery routes based on real-time traffic data, reducing fuel consumption and improving delivery times. These operational improvements, driven by AI insights, can significantly enhance a company's bottom line.

2.4 Data Governance and Ethical Considerations

While the potential of AI to leverage data for insights is vast, businesses must also be mindful of the ethical and governance challenges associated with data usage. With the increasing reliance on data comes the responsibility to ensure that it is collected, stored, and used ethically. **Data privacy** is a major concern, as customers become more aware of how their personal information is being used. Businesses that fail to handle data responsibly risk losing consumer trust, facing regulatory penalties, and damaging their reputations.

AI introduces additional complexities when it comes to data governance. For instance, AI models can sometimes perpetuate biases present in the data they are trained on, leading to discriminatory outcomes. To address these challenges, businesses must invest in **AI transparency** and **explainability**. Explainable AI (XAI) refers to systems that provide clear, understandable explanations of how decisions are made, helping businesses ensure that AI-driven insights are fair, unbiased, and transparent. Additionally, organizations must establish robust **data governance frameworks**, including data quality control, privacy compliance, and ethical guidelines for AI development and deployment.

2.5 The Strategic Advantage of Data and AI Integration

The integration of data and AI provides businesses with a significant strategic advantage, as it enables them to operate more efficiently, make informed decisions, and innovate rapidly. Companies that successfully harness AI to leverage their data are not only better positioned to understand their customers and markets, but they can also anticipate changes and adapt quickly. In a fast-moving digital economy, the ability to turn data into actionable insights in real time is a powerful differentiator that can drive long-term success.

Looking ahead, the value of data and AI will only continue to grow as more industries adopt AI-powered technologies and generate even larger datasets. Companies that embrace AI as a critical component of their data strategy will be at the forefront of innovation, able to capitalize on emerging opportunities and navigate the complexities of a data-driven world. The future belongs to businesses that understand that data, combined with AI, is not just a tool but the key to unlocking new value, driving competitive advantage, and shaping the future of industry.

4o

2.1 AI's Role in Data Collection and Processing

Artificial intelligence (AI) has transformed how businesses collect, process, and analyze data, making it faster, more efficient, and scalable. With the sheer volume of data being generated daily by digital transactions, connected devices, social media, and sensors, traditional methods of data collection and processing are no longer sufficient. AI has emerged as a powerful tool that not only automates these tasks but also enhances their accuracy and depth, allowing organizations to derive valuable insights from vast datasets. AI's ability to handle both structured and unstructured data with precision has made it an indispensable asset in the data-driven economy.

The Shift Toward Automated Data Collection

Data collection, once a manual and labor-intensive process, is now largely automated through AI-driven systems. These systems have revolutionized how businesses gather data, allowing them to collect information from a wide array of sources—ranging from transactional databases and customer interactions to external web data, social media, IoT devices, and more.

One of the key technologies in automated data collection is **machine learning**. Machine learning algorithms can sift through massive datasets, identify patterns, and learn from the data, continually improving how they collect and categorize information. For example, e-commerce platforms use machine learning to track customer behavior, automatically logging every click, purchase, and interaction across websites and apps. This data is collected in real-time, providing a continuous stream of insights without the need for human intervention.

Another major development in data collection is the use of **natural language processing (NLP)**, which enables businesses to gather and analyze unstructured data from text sources like customer reviews, emails, and social media posts. NLP tools can scan and extract meaning from large amounts of textual data, identifying key sentiments, topics, and trends. This capability is particularly important in industries like retail, where customer sentiment and feedback can inform product development and marketing strategies.

AI is also instrumental in gathering data from **sensor networks and IoT devices**. The proliferation of IoT devices has created new data sources, such as smart home devices, wearables, and industrial sensors. AI systems can collect, analyze, and act on this data in real-time, enabling businesses to monitor and optimize processes without manual oversight. For example, in manufacturing, AI-driven systems collect data from machines on the factory floor, tracking performance and identifying signs of wear or failure. This continuous data collection helps organizations move from reactive to proactive maintenance, reducing downtime and increasing efficiency.

Efficient Data Processing Through AI

The vast amount of data collected from multiple sources requires sophisticated processing to extract meaningful insights. Traditional data processing systems, which rely on predefined models and manual analysis, are often overwhelmed by the volume, variety, and velocity of modern data. AI, particularly through machine learning and deep learning techniques, has proven capable of handling this challenge by automating and optimizing the processing of complex datasets.

One of the key advantages AI offers in data processing is its ability to work with both **structured and unstructured data**. Structured data, which is organized into rows and columns (e.g., spreadsheets, databases), can be processed relatively easily by traditional systems. However, unstructured data, which includes text, images, audio, and video, requires more advanced processing techniques. AI-powered tools, such as **image recognition** and **speech-to-text** algorithms, can efficiently process unstructured data and extract useful information. For instance, AI can automatically categorize and tag images based on their content, making it easier for businesses to organize and analyze large collections of visual data.

AI also excels at handling **real-time data processing**. In today's fast-paced business environment, organizations often need to process data as it is generated, allowing them to make quick decisions and respond to changes in the market. AI enables real-time processing by using **edge computing** and cloud-based platforms to analyze data at its source, reducing latency and enabling faster decision-making. For example, financial institutions use AI-driven systems to process and analyze real-time stock market data, allowing traders to make split-second decisions based on evolving market conditions.

Another area where AI is transforming data processing is through **predictive analytics**. AI algorithms can analyze historical data to predict future trends, behaviors, and outcomes. This allows businesses to process data in a way that not only informs them of past performance but also provides insights into what may happen next. In sectors such as retail, healthcare, and manufacturing, predictive analytics driven by AI helps organizations anticipate demand, optimize supply chains, and improve customer service.

Data Cleansing and Preparation Through AI

Before data can be effectively used for decision-making, it must be cleaned, organized, and prepared for analysis—a process known as **data preprocessing**. Raw data is often messy, containing inconsistencies, duplicates, errors, and missing values. In the past, data preparation was a time-consuming task requiring significant human intervention.

AI has automated much of this process, allowing businesses to process data faster and more accurately.

AI-driven tools can automatically detect and correct errors in datasets, such as duplicate entries or incorrect values, ensuring that the data is clean and reliable. **Machine learning** models can also identify outliers or anomalies in data that may skew analysis results. For example, AI systems used in fraud detection can flag suspicious transactions by analyzing large volumes of transaction data and spotting patterns that deviate from the norm.

In addition to cleansing data, AI can also assist in **data enrichment**. This involves augmenting a dataset with additional information from external sources to enhance its value. For instance, AI can enrich customer data by linking it to external databases, providing insights into customer demographics, preferences, or behavior patterns. This enriched data can then be used to build more accurate predictive models and drive better decision-making.

Furthermore, AI improves **data integration**, a critical step in combining data from multiple sources. With businesses collecting data from a variety of platforms—such as CRM systems, social media, and third-party databases—AI helps streamline the process of merging these diverse datasets into a single, unified view. AI algorithms can automate data mapping, matching, and consolidation, reducing the time and effort required for manual data integration.

Scaling Data Collection and Processing with AI

As businesses grow and the volume of data they generate increases, scalability becomes a critical concern. AI enables organizations to scale their data collection and processing efforts seamlessly, regardless of the size or complexity of the data. AI-powered systems can handle **big data** environments, processing large datasets efficiently and effectively, without the need for massive infrastructure investments.

Cloud-based AI solutions are a key enabler of scalable data processing. Many businesses are adopting cloud platforms that offer AI capabilities, allowing them to store and process vast amounts of data without having to invest in on-premises hardware. These platforms provide access to powerful AI tools for data collection, analysis, and visualization, enabling businesses of all sizes to harness the power of AI. For example, a company can use cloud-based AI services to analyze customer data from multiple sources, gain insights into purchasing behavior, and optimize marketing strategies in real time.

AI-driven data processing also scales through **automation**. As AI systems learn and improve over time, they require less human intervention, allowing businesses to manage larger datasets and more complex processes without additional manpower. For example, AI can automate the processing of financial reports, customer feedback, or social media data, providing insights continuously without the need for constant human oversight.

Challenges in AI-Driven Data Collection and Processing

While AI offers numerous advantages in data collection and processing, businesses must be aware of the challenges associated with its use. One of the primary challenges is **data quality**. AI systems rely on high-quality data to function effectively. If the data fed into AI systems is incomplete, outdated, or biased, it can lead to inaccurate insights and flawed decision-making. Ensuring that data is properly cleansed, labeled, and formatted is essential for AI to perform optimally.

Another challenge is related to **data privacy and security**. As businesses collect more data, particularly personal or sensitive information, they must comply with regulations such as the **General Data Protection Regulation (GDPR)** and the **California Consumer Privacy Act (CCPA)**. AI systems that collect and process data must be designed to handle privacy concerns, ensuring that data is anonymized and stored securely to protect against breaches and misuse.

In conclusion, AI has fundamentally changed how businesses collect and process data, offering greater speed, accuracy, and scalability. By automating the collection of data from diverse sources and optimizing its processing, AI enables organizations to gain deeper insights, drive better decision-making, and remain competitive in the data-driven economy. However, businesses must also address the challenges associated with data quality, privacy, and ethical considerations to fully realize the potential of AI in data collection and processing.

2.2 Data Analytics and Predictive Modeling

Data analytics and predictive modeling have become cornerstones of business intelligence, offering companies the ability to transform raw data into actionable insights and accurate forecasts. With the integration of artificial intelligence (AI), these processes have become more advanced, efficient, and scalable. AI-driven analytics allow businesses to not only understand historical trends but also predict future outcomes, enabling proactive decision-making. In this section, we will explore how AI enhances data analytics, the role of predictive modeling, and how these capabilities can be harnessed to drive business success.

The Role of Data Analytics in Business

Data analytics refers to the process of examining datasets to draw conclusions about the information they contain. Traditionally, data analytics was limited to historical data, where businesses would analyze past performance to understand trends, measure KPIs, and identify areas for improvement. While this descriptive analytics approach provided valuable insights, it was inherently reactive—decisions were made after events occurred, rather than in anticipation of future trends.

With the advent of AI, data analytics has evolved to include predictive and prescriptive analytics. AI-driven analytics can now process vast amounts of data in real-time, providing not only a retrospective view of performance but also forward-looking insights that help businesses stay ahead of the curve. These insights come from the ability of AI algorithms to detect patterns in data, uncover relationships, and learn from past behavior to predict future outcomes.

AI enhances data analytics in several ways:

- **Speed and Scale**: AI can analyze large datasets at a speed and scale far beyond human capacity. Machine learning algorithms can sift through vast amounts of data from multiple sources, processing it in real-time to deliver insights almost instantaneously.
- **Accuracy**: AI reduces the risk of human error in data analysis by automating the process and using sophisticated models that can detect patterns and correlations in data that may be missed by manual analysis.
- **Real-time Decision Making**: With the ability to process data continuously, AI-powered analytics allows businesses to make decisions in real time. For example, financial institutions use real-time analytics to monitor market conditions and adjust

trading strategies instantly, while e-commerce platforms analyze customer behavior in real time to personalize user experiences.

Types of Data Analytics

To understand the value of AI in data analytics, it's essential to recognize the different types of analytics that businesses use:

1. **Descriptive Analytics**: This is the most basic form of analytics, focusing on summarizing historical data to understand what happened in the past. Descriptive analytics provides insights into trends, patterns, and anomalies in data. While it does not predict future outcomes, it offers a comprehensive overview of past performance, which can be useful for setting benchmarks and goals.

2. **Diagnostic Analytics**: Building on descriptive analytics, diagnostic analytics aims to explain why something happened. This involves digging deeper into data to identify the root causes of trends or anomalies. AI can enhance diagnostic analytics by automatically correlating various data points and identifying relationships that may not be

immediately apparent, helping businesses understand the underlying factors driving performance.

3. **Predictive Analytics**: Predictive analytics uses historical data to forecast future outcomes. Machine learning models analyze past behavior, detect patterns, and use that information to predict what is likely to happen next. This type of analytics is invaluable for businesses looking to anticipate customer demand, market shifts, or operational risks.

4. **Prescriptive Analytics**: Going beyond prediction, prescriptive analytics provides recommendations on the best course of action based on data-driven insights. AI-powered prescriptive analytics can optimize decision-making by suggesting strategies that will lead to the desired outcomes. For example, AI might recommend specific marketing campaigns that are likely to resonate with a particular audience based on past performance and current trends.

Predictive Modeling: Forecasting the Future with AI

Predictive modeling is the process of using historical data to build models that forecast future outcomes. AI, particularly machine learning, has revolutionized predictive modeling by automating the development and refinement of these models, enabling businesses to generate accurate predictions with minimal human intervention.

At the heart of predictive modeling are **machine learning algorithms**, which can be trained to recognize patterns and relationships within data. These models are typically built using supervised learning, where the algorithm is trained on a labeled dataset (where the outcome is known) and then used to make predictions on new, unseen data.

Common types of machine learning algorithms used in predictive modeling include:

- **Regression Analysis**: Regression models are used to predict continuous outcomes, such as sales figures or stock prices, based on the relationships between variables. Linear regression is one of the simplest forms of predictive modeling, but AI can enhance this approach by using more advanced techniques like polynomial regression, decision trees, or random forests, which can capture more complex relationships in data.

- **Classification Models**: Classification models predict categorical outcomes, such as whether a customer will churn or not, or whether a transaction is fraudulent. Algorithms such as **logistic regression**, **support vector machines (SVM)**, and **neural networks** are commonly used for classification tasks.

- **Time Series Forecasting**: Time series forecasting models predict future values based on historical time-based data. AI enhances traditional time series models by using deep learning techniques such as **recurrent neural networks (RNNs)**, which are particularly effective for predicting sequences and trends over time.

AI-Driven Predictive Models in Action

AI-driven predictive models have wide-ranging applications across industries, helping businesses forecast outcomes, anticipate customer needs, and optimize operations.

1. **Retail and E-Commerce**: In retail, predictive modeling powered by AI is used to forecast customer demand, optimize inventory, and

personalize marketing efforts. By analyzing past purchasing behavior, search history, and demographic data, AI can predict which products customers are likely to buy, when they are most likely to make a purchase, and what factors influence their decision-making. Retailers can then use these insights to adjust pricing, manage stock levels, and launch targeted promotions, resulting in increased sales and reduced waste.

2. **Financial Services**: In the financial sector, AI-driven predictive models are used for risk management, fraud detection, and investment forecasting. For example, predictive models can analyze historical transaction data to identify patterns indicative of fraud, flagging suspicious activities in real time. Similarly, financial institutions use predictive models to assess credit risk by analyzing customer financial histories, enabling more accurate lending decisions.

3. **Healthcare**: AI-powered predictive modeling is transforming healthcare by enabling early disease detection, personalized treatment plans, and improved patient outcomes. Predictive models can analyze patient data—such as medical records,

genetic information, and lifestyle factors—to predict the likelihood of certain diseases or conditions. For example, AI models can predict the likelihood of readmission for patients based on their health history, allowing healthcare providers to intervene early and prevent costly hospital readmissions.

4. **Manufacturing and Supply Chain**: In manufacturing, predictive modeling is used for **predictive maintenance**, which involves using sensor data to predict when machinery is likely to fail. By analyzing historical maintenance records and real-time performance data, AI models can predict equipment failures before they happen, allowing companies to perform maintenance proactively and avoid costly downtime. Similarly, predictive models in supply chain management help companies forecast demand and optimize logistics, ensuring timely deliveries and reducing excess inventory.

5. **Marketing and Customer Engagement**: Predictive models are widely used in marketing to anticipate customer behavior and improve engagement. AI-driven models can predict which

customers are likely to churn, allowing businesses to take preemptive action to retain them through targeted offers and personalized communications. Additionally, AI can analyze customer data to predict their lifetime value (CLV), enabling companies to allocate resources more effectively and focus on high-value customers.

Building and Refining Predictive Models

Creating effective predictive models requires several steps, including data collection, model selection, training, and validation. AI simplifies and automates many aspects of this process, but human oversight remains critical to ensure models are accurate, unbiased, and ethical.

1. **Data Collection and Preparation**: The first step in building a predictive model is gathering relevant data. This data must be clean, accurate, and representative of the problem being addressed. AI-powered tools can automate much of the data cleaning process by identifying and correcting errors, filling in missing values, and transforming raw data into a usable format.

2. **Model Selection**: Choosing the right model depends on the type of problem being solved and the nature of the data. For instance, regression models are suited for predicting continuous variables, while classification models are used for categorical outcomes. AI can assist in this process by using **automated machine learning (AutoML)**, which automatically selects the best model based on the dataset and desired outcome.

3. **Training and Validation**: Once a model is selected, it must be trained on a labeled dataset to learn the relationships between variables. AI can optimize this process by using techniques such as **cross-validation**, which evaluates the model's performance on different subsets of data to ensure it generalizes well to new data. AI systems also use **hyperparameter tuning** to automatically adjust model settings and improve accuracy.

4. **Model Refinement**: After training, predictive models are tested and refined based on their performance. AI enables continuous model improvement through **reinforcement learning**, where models learn from their predictions and

outcomes, adjusting their parameters over time to improve accuracy.

Challenges and Ethical Considerations

While AI-driven predictive modeling offers powerful benefits, there are also challenges and ethical considerations to address. One major concern is the potential for **bias** in predictive models. If the data used to train a model contains historical biases, the model may perpetuate these biases in its predictions. For example, if a predictive model used in hiring decisions is trained on biased data, it may unfairly discriminate against certain candidates based on gender, race, or other factors. Ensuring that models are trained on representative and unbiased data is critical to maintaining fairness and transparency.

Another challenge is **data privacy**. Predictive models often rely on personal and sensitive data to make accurate predictions, raising concerns about how this data is collected, stored, and used. Businesses must comply with privacy regulations like the **GDPR** and **CCPA**, ensuring that customers' data is protected and used ethically.

In conclusion, AI-powered data analytics and predictive modeling have transformed how businesses leverage data to make informed decisions. By automating data analysis and using machine learning to forecast future outcomes, businesses can gain a competitive edge, optimize operations, and improve customer experiences. However, organizations must be mindful of the ethical implications of AI and take steps to ensure their models are fair, unbiased, and transparent.

2.3 Enhancing Business Intelligence through AI

Artificial intelligence (AI) has revolutionized business intelligence (BI), transforming it from a traditional data reporting system into an advanced tool for real-time insights, strategic decision-making, and proactive problem-solving. In the digital age, data is often considered the most valuable asset, but without the tools to process, analyze, and derive insights from it, data can be overwhelming. AI enhances business intelligence by enabling businesses to unlock the full potential of their data, allowing them to respond faster to market changes, optimize operations, and improve customer experiences.

This section explores how AI improves BI processes, the technologies involved, and the significant benefits it offers in today's data-driven business environment.

The Evolution of Business Intelligence

Historically, business intelligence was focused on generating reports and dashboards based on historical data. These reports allowed businesses to track key performance indicators (KPIs), monitor financials, and review past performance. However, traditional BI systems were limited in scope, primarily providing descriptive analytics—data summaries that answered questions like "What happened?" and "How did we perform?"

The integration of AI into BI has shifted this paradigm from descriptive to **predictive** and **prescriptive analytics**, enabling businesses to not only understand past events but also anticipate future outcomes and optimize their strategies. This evolution has been driven by advances in machine learning, natural language processing, and data automation, which allow businesses to move beyond static reports toward dynamic, real-time insights that can transform decision-making processes.

Key Technologies Enhancing Business Intelligence through AI

AI-driven BI systems leverage a variety of technologies to enhance data analysis, visualization, and decision-making. These technologies work together to automate data processing, extract meaningful insights, and deliver actionable intelligence.

1. **Machine Learning (ML)**: Machine learning algorithms are the backbone of AI-enhanced BI. By training on historical data, ML models can recognize patterns, correlations, and trends in data, allowing them to make predictions about future events. For instance, a machine learning model can predict sales trends based on customer behavior, economic conditions, and past purchasing patterns. These predictions help businesses optimize inventory, pricing strategies, and marketing efforts.

2. **Natural Language Processing (NLP)**: NLP allows BI tools to interpret and analyze unstructured data, such as text from social media posts, customer reviews, emails, and other non-numeric sources. With NLP, AI-powered BI systems can extract sentiment, identify key topics, and provide insights

into customer preferences and trends. Moreover, NLP enables natural language queries, allowing business users to interact with BI systems using everyday language. For example, a user might ask, "What were our top-selling products last quarter?" and receive a detailed response in both data and narrative form.

3. **Automated Data Processing**: One of the most significant advantages of AI in BI is the automation of data collection, cleansing, and integration. AI can automatically extract data from multiple sources— internal databases, cloud platforms, third-party APIs, social media, etc.—and transform it into a unified format, saving time and reducing errors. This automation ensures that businesses have access to accurate, up-to-date data without the need for manual intervention, improving the quality of insights derived from BI systems.

4. **Real-time Data Analytics**: Traditional BI systems often work with static, historical data, producing reports based on information from the past. AI, combined with real-time data streaming technologies, allows businesses to analyze and respond to data as it is generated. This real-time

capability is particularly important in industries like finance, where stock prices, market conditions, and trading volumes fluctuate constantly. By leveraging AI for real-time analysis, businesses can make timely decisions that capitalize on emerging opportunities or mitigate risks.

5. **Data Visualization and Dashboards**: AI-powered BI tools are equipped with advanced data visualization capabilities, making it easier for business users to interpret complex datasets. Machine learning algorithms can automatically identify the most relevant data points and recommend the best visualizations, such as graphs, charts, or heatmaps. Interactive dashboards powered by AI allow users to drill down into data and explore trends without requiring in-depth technical expertise. These visualizations provide an intuitive and engaging way to understand data, making it easier to identify actionable insights.

AI's Impact on Decision-Making

AI-enhanced BI systems go beyond simply reporting on past performance; they actively contribute to decision-making by providing actionable insights and strategic recommendations. This capability can fundamentally change how businesses operate, offering several key benefits:

1. **Proactive Problem-Solving**: Traditional BI systems primarily focus on analyzing past data, helping businesses understand what has already happened. AI takes this a step further by predicting future trends and identifying potential problems before they occur. For instance, an AI-driven BI system could alert a company to an upcoming inventory shortage based on real-time sales data, allowing them to adjust orders and prevent stockouts. Similarly, predictive maintenance models can analyze machine data to forecast equipment failures, enabling proactive maintenance scheduling and reducing costly downtime.

2. **Personalized Customer Experiences**: In today's highly competitive market, businesses must tailor their offerings to individual customer preferences. AI-enhanced BI can analyze customer data, such as purchase history, browsing behavior, and engagement metrics, to create personalized recommendations and offers. This personalization helps improve customer satisfaction and increases

revenue by offering relevant products or services at the right time. For example, e-commerce platforms use AI to analyze customer behavior in real-time, delivering product recommendations based on browsing habits, previous purchases, and similar customer profiles.

3. **Data-Driven Strategic Planning**: AI-driven BI systems provide deeper insights that can inform long-term business strategies. By analyzing market trends, customer behavior, and operational data, AI can help businesses identify growth opportunities, optimize resource allocation, and make informed decisions about future investments. For instance, AI-powered predictive models can forecast changes in customer demand, allowing companies to adjust production schedules and inventory levels accordingly. Similarly, businesses can use AI insights to develop new products or services based on emerging trends and customer needs.

4. **Operational Efficiency**: AI-enhanced BI tools streamline business processes by automating routine tasks and optimizing decision-making. For example, AI can analyze operational data to identify bottlenecks in supply chains or inefficiencies in

production workflows, allowing businesses to take corrective actions. Additionally, AI-driven prescriptive analytics can recommend specific actions to improve performance, such as adjusting staffing levels, reallocating resources, or modifying production schedules. By automating decision-making processes, businesses can reduce costs, improve productivity, and maintain a competitive edge.

5. **Enhanced Risk Management**: Risk management is critical in industries such as finance, healthcare, and manufacturing, where mistakes can have significant financial or operational consequences. AI-powered BI systems can help organizations identify and mitigate risks by analyzing data patterns that may indicate potential issues. For example, in the financial sector, AI models can assess credit risk by analyzing a borrower's financial history, flagging high-risk loans, or predicting defaults. In manufacturing, AI-driven systems can analyze equipment data to detect early signs of failure, reducing the risk of accidents or costly downtime.

Self-Service Business Intelligence

One of the most transformative aspects of AI-enhanced BI is the rise of **self-service BI**, which empowers non-technical users to interact with data and gain insights without relying on data analysts or IT teams. In traditional BI systems, extracting insights from data required specialized knowledge of databases, query languages, and data visualization tools. AI has democratized access to BI, allowing business users to generate reports, explore data, and ask questions using natural language or intuitive interfaces.

With AI-driven self-service BI, users can:

- **Create their own reports and dashboards** by selecting relevant data points and applying filters, without needing technical skills.
- **Interact with AI chatbots or virtual assistants**, asking questions about business performance in natural language and receiving responses in the form of charts, graphs, or narratives.
- **Customize insights based on their specific needs**, tailoring data visualizations and reports to their department, role, or objectives.

Self-service BI enhances organizational agility by reducing reliance on centralized data teams, allowing employees across departments to access data-driven insights and make informed decisions more quickly.

Challenges and Considerations for AI in Business Intelligence

While AI offers immense benefits to business intelligence, there are also challenges and considerations to keep in mind when implementing AI-powered BI systems:

1. **Data Quality**: AI systems rely heavily on data to generate insights, so the quality and accuracy of data are critical. If the data fed into the system is incomplete, inconsistent, or biased, the AI-driven insights may be flawed. Businesses must invest in robust data governance frameworks to ensure that their data is clean, accurate, and reliable.

2. **Data Privacy and Security**: As businesses collect and analyze more data, particularly personal and sensitive information, they must navigate complex privacy regulations such as the **General Data Protection Regulation (GDPR)** and the **California Consumer Privacy Act (CCPA)**. AI-powered BI

systems must be designed with privacy in mind, ensuring that data is anonymized, protected, and used in compliance with relevant regulations.

3. **Integration with Existing Systems**: AI-driven BI systems often require integration with existing databases, cloud platforms, and third-party tools. Ensuring seamless integration across diverse data sources can be challenging, particularly for organizations with legacy systems. Businesses must invest in scalable and flexible BI platforms that can integrate with their existing infrastructure and support future growth.

4. **Ethical Considerations**: As AI plays a larger role in business decision-making, companies must address the ethical implications of using AI-driven insights. This includes ensuring that AI algorithms are transparent, fair, and free from bias. Additionally, businesses must consider the impact of AI-driven decisions on employees, customers, and society as a whole.

The Future of AI in Business Intelligence

The future of business intelligence lies in the continued integration of AI and emerging technologies like **deep** learning, **cognitive computing**, and **augmented analytics**. As AI algorithms become more sophisticated, BI systems will increasingly be able to process unstructured data (

2.4 Turning Big Data into Actionable Insights

In today's hyper-connected world, businesses generate and collect massive amounts of data—often referred to as **big data**. This data comes from various sources, including customer interactions, social media, sensors in IoT devices, financial transactions, and operational systems. While big data offers immense opportunities for organizations, it also presents significant challenges. The sheer volume, velocity, and variety of data can overwhelm traditional business intelligence (BI) systems, making it difficult for businesses to extract meaningful insights. This is where **AI** plays a transformative role, turning raw data into actionable insights that drive business strategy, improve operations, and enhance customer experiences.

The Characteristics of Big Data

Big data is often defined by the **three Vs**:

- **Volume**: The scale of data being generated is enormous. Businesses today collect data from an expanding range of sources, including websites, mobile apps, social media, and sensors. The amount of data generated globally is growing exponentially, and businesses need advanced tools to manage and process this volume of information.

- **Velocity**: Data is being generated at unprecedented speeds. In industries like finance or e-commerce, new data points are produced every second, requiring real-time analysis and decision-making. Traditional systems are often unable to keep pace with this velocity, making it difficult to respond to rapidly changing market conditions.

- **Variety**: Data comes in multiple formats, including structured data (like databases and spreadsheets), semi-structured data (like XML or JSON files), and unstructured data (like images, videos, emails, and social media posts). The diversity of data types presents challenges in storage, processing, and analysis.

Beyond these, **veracity** (the trustworthiness of data) and **value** (the actionable insights derived from it) are also critical aspects of big data. Without the right tools and strategies, businesses can easily find themselves buried under mountains of data without gaining any valuable insights.

AI's Role in Analyzing Big Data

AI technologies, including **machine learning (ML)**, **natural language processing (NLP)**, and **deep learning**, have the capacity to process, analyze, and learn from vast amounts of data far more effectively than traditional BI systems. These technologies allow businesses to sift through enormous datasets, identify patterns and correlations, and generate predictive and prescriptive insights that are actionable.

Here's how AI enhances big data analytics and turns it into valuable business insights:

1. **Automating Data Processing**: One of the major challenges of big data is the time and effort required to process it. AI algorithms can automatically ingest, clean, and organize data from diverse sources, drastically reducing the time it takes to prepare data for analysis. AI tools can also identify and correct data inconsistencies, such as duplicate

records or missing information, improving the accuracy of subsequent analyses.

2. **Advanced Pattern Recognition**: AI excels at identifying patterns and correlations in complex datasets that would be impossible or time-consuming for human analysts to detect. Machine learning algorithms can analyze customer purchasing behavior, social media trends, or website traffic to uncover hidden patterns, such as which products are most popular among certain demographics or how external factors like weather or economic conditions influence sales. These insights help businesses optimize their marketing, sales, and operational strategies.

3. **Scalability**: Traditional data processing tools often struggle to handle the massive scale of big data. AI, on the other hand, is designed to scale, leveraging cloud computing and distributed processing frameworks to manage data on a petabyte (or larger) scale. This allows businesses to analyze entire datasets, rather than relying on smaller samples, leading to more comprehensive and accurate insights.

4. **Real-time Analysis**: In industries where immediate decision-making is critical—such as finance, healthcare, or e-commerce—AI allows businesses to analyze data in real-time. For example, AI-powered fraud detection systems can monitor financial transactions as they occur, flagging suspicious activity and preventing fraudulent transactions before they are completed. Similarly, e-commerce platforms can use real-time data to adjust pricing, recommend products, or tailor promotions based on a customer's current browsing behavior.

5. **Predictive and Prescriptive Analytics**: Beyond simply reporting on historical data, AI-driven analytics allows businesses to predict future outcomes and recommend actions to optimize those outcomes. For example, predictive maintenance models can analyze data from IoT sensors to forecast when machinery is likely to fail, allowing companies to perform maintenance before a breakdown occurs. Prescriptive analytics goes one step further, recommending specific actions based on predictive insights. For example, a retail company might use prescriptive analytics to

determine the optimal inventory levels based on predicted customer demand during holiday seasons.

Steps to Turn Big Data into Actionable Insights

Successfully transforming big data into actionable insights involves several key steps, from data collection to decision-making. Here's how AI supports this process:

1. **Data Collection**: The first step is gathering relevant data from internal and external sources. AI plays a crucial role in automating data collection from diverse sources such as CRM systems, social media platforms, IoT devices, and external APIs. AI can also monitor these data sources continuously, ensuring that the organization has up-to-date information.

2. **Data Integration and Cleansing**: Data from different sources often comes in varying formats and may contain errors or inconsistencies. AI tools automate the process of integrating this data into a unified system, removing duplicates, filling in missing values, and transforming it into a format suitable for analysis. This step is critical to ensure

the quality of the data and the reliability of the insights derived from it.

3. **Data Analysis**: Once the data is clean and ready for analysis, AI algorithms analyze it to extract insights. This could involve anything from running simple statistical models to applying complex machine learning techniques like clustering, classification, or regression. AI can also identify relationships between variables that may not be immediately apparent, such as how weather patterns affect customer foot traffic or how economic conditions influence purchasing behavior.

4. **Visualization and Reporting**: AI-powered business intelligence tools often come with advanced data visualization features, allowing businesses to represent complex datasets through charts, graphs, heatmaps, or dashboards. These visualizations help stakeholders quickly understand key trends and insights. Interactive dashboards powered by AI allow users to drill down into specific data points, exploring trends in more detail.

5. **Decision-Making and Action**: The ultimate goal of analyzing big data is to inform business decisions. AI-driven insights can help businesses take specific

actions, such as optimizing supply chain operations, personalizing marketing campaigns, or developing new products based on customer feedback. These actions can then be measured for effectiveness, creating a feedback loop where AI continues to learn from new data and refine its recommendations.

Real-World Applications of Turning Big Data into Actionable Insights

1. **Retail and E-commerce**: Retailers can use AI to analyze data from customer interactions, sales, and inventory management systems. By understanding purchasing trends, customer preferences, and external factors like seasonality, businesses can make data-driven decisions about which products to promote, when to adjust pricing, and how to optimize supply chain operations. AI-powered recommendation engines also use big data to suggest products to customers, boosting sales and enhancing the shopping experience.

2. **Healthcare**: In healthcare, big data can be used to improve patient outcomes by analyzing data from electronic health records (EHRs), medical devices,

and clinical trials. AI algorithms can identify patterns in patient data that may indicate early warning signs of diseases, such as cancer or diabetes, allowing for earlier diagnosis and treatment. Healthcare providers can also use AI to optimize resource allocation, ensuring that hospitals and clinics have the right number of staff and equipment based on predicted patient demand.

3. **Finance**: The finance industry leverages big data and AI to manage risk, detect fraud, and improve investment strategies. For example, banks use AI to analyze transaction data and detect patterns that suggest fraudulent activity. Hedge funds and investment firms use AI to analyze financial data and news to predict stock prices and make more informed investment decisions.

4. **Manufacturing**: In manufacturing, AI-driven analytics can optimize production processes by analyzing data from sensors on factory floors. Predictive maintenance models help manufacturers anticipate equipment failures before they occur, reducing downtime and maintenance costs. AI also helps manufacturers optimize supply chain

operations by analyzing data on raw materials, production schedules, and demand forecasts.

Challenges in Turning Big Data into Actionable Insights

1. **Data Silos**: One of the biggest challenges businesses face is dealing with data silos, where data is stored in disparate systems or departments. AI can help break down these silos by integrating data from various sources, but businesses must invest in infrastructure that supports seamless data sharing.

2. **Data Privacy and Compliance**: As businesses collect more data, they must navigate increasingly complex regulations like the **General Data Protection Regulation (GDPR)** and **California Consumer Privacy Act (CCPA)**. AI systems must be designed to handle data in compliance with these regulations, ensuring that personal information is protected and used ethically.

3. **Skills Gap**: While AI offers powerful tools for turning big data into actionable insights, many organizations lack the in-house expertise to implement and manage AI-driven systems. Businesses need to invest in training or hire data

scientists and AI experts to fully leverage these technologies.

4. **Data Quality**: The value of AI insights is only as good as the quality of the data being analyzed. Incomplete, inaccurate, or biased data can lead to flawed conclusions. Businesses must prioritize data quality through robust data governance practices, ensuring that the data they collect is accurate, complete, and relevant.

Turning big data into actionable insights is essential for businesses looking to remain competitive in the digital age. AI plays a critical role in this process, automating data collection and processing, identifying patterns and trends, and providing real-time insights that drive decision-making. However, to fully leverage the power of big data and AI, businesses must invest in the right infrastructure, tools, and expertise, while also addressing challenges such as

2.5 Overcoming Data Challenges: Privacy, Security, and Bias

As businesses increasingly rely on big data and artificial intelligence (AI) to drive decision-making, they face a growing set of challenges related to data privacy, security, and bias. These issues are critical not only for ensuring the integrity and fairness of AI-driven insights but also for building and maintaining trust with customers, stakeholders, and regulatory bodies. While the potential of data to transform businesses is immense, mismanagement or misuse of data can lead to significant financial, legal, and reputational consequences. In this section, we explore these three major challenges in detail and discuss strategies for overcoming them.

Data Privacy: Navigating Complex Regulations and Ethical Use of Data

In today's digital landscape, businesses collect vast amounts of personal and sensitive data, from customer preferences and buying habits to medical records and financial transactions. However, with this growing data collection comes an increasing responsibility to protect individuals' privacy. Data privacy refers to the rights of individuals to control how their personal information is collected, used, shared, and stored. Ensuring data privacy is critical for complying with regulatory frameworks, such as the **General Data Protection Regulation (GDPR)** in Europe, the **California Consumer Privacy Act (CCPA)** in the United States, and similar laws in other regions. These regulations place strict requirements on how businesses must handle personal data, with severe penalties for non-compliance.

One of the key challenges in managing data privacy is balancing the need for data-driven insights with respect for individual privacy rights. AI systems often require vast datasets to function effectively, particularly for training machine learning models. However, much of this data can include personally identifiable information (PII) or sensitive details that could be misused if not properly protected. To overcome these challenges, businesses must implement robust privacy policies and adopt **privacy-by-design** principles, ensuring that privacy considerations are embedded into every stage of data collection, storage, and analysis.

Data anonymization and **pseudonymization** techniques are common strategies used to protect privacy while still allowing for valuable data insights. Anonymization removes any identifiable information from the data, making it impossible to trace back to an individual. Pseudonymization replaces identifiable information with artificial identifiers or pseudonyms, offering a layer of privacy while still allowing for data analysis. However, even these techniques must be carefully applied, as sophisticated algorithms could re-identify individuals by correlating anonymized data with external datasets. As a result, businesses must ensure that any de-anonymization risks are minimized through ongoing monitoring and testing.

Moreover, organizations need to ensure **data transparency** by informing customers about what data is being collected, how it will be used, and who will have access to it. Consent management is essential, where businesses give customers clear options to opt in or out of data collection and provide tools to manage their privacy preferences. Additionally, implementing data minimization practices—collecting only the data that is necessary for specific purposes—can reduce the risks associated with data breaches or misuse.

Data Security: Safeguarding Against Breaches and Cyber Threats

With the increasing volume of data collected by businesses comes a heightened risk of data breaches and cyberattacks. **Data security** refers to the processes and technologies designed to protect sensitive information from unauthorized access, theft, or damage. As organizations accumulate vast amounts of data, they become more attractive targets for hackers and cybercriminals. A data breach can result in significant financial losses, regulatory fines, and damage to a company's reputation, especially if sensitive information, such as credit card numbers, social security details, or health records, is exposed.

Securing data involves implementing **strong encryption** protocols, both in transit and at rest. Encryption ensures that even if data is intercepted by unauthorized parties, it cannot be easily read or used. Businesses should also adopt **multi-factor authentication (MFA)** and **role-based access controls (RBAC)** to limit access to sensitive data to only those employees or systems that require it. These measures reduce the risk of internal threats, where unauthorized individuals within the organization gain access to data they should not have.

Another essential component of data security is maintaining a robust **cybersecurity infrastructure** that includes firewalls, intrusion detection systems, and regular vulnerability assessments. AI itself can play a role in enhancing data security by identifying unusual patterns in network traffic, detecting potential threats in real time, and responding to attacks before they cause significant harm. For example, AI-driven security systems can flag suspicious login attempts or detect malware embedded in email attachments before they reach end users.

However, the biggest challenge in data security is the human factor. **Phishing attacks**, where hackers trick employees into revealing passwords or downloading malware, remain one of the most common ways data breaches occur. To overcome this, businesses must invest in regular cybersecurity training for their employees, ensuring that they are aware of common threats and know how to respond to potential security incidents. Moreover, implementing **data backup** and **disaster recovery** plans ensures that businesses can recover quickly in the event of a data breach or system failure, minimizing downtime and preventing data loss.

Another challenge that businesses must navigate is the secure sharing of data with third parties, such as vendors, partners, or cloud service providers. When sharing data across multiple entities, ensuring that all parties adhere to stringent security standards is critical to preventing breaches. **Data encryption**, **contractual agreements**, and **regular audits** are essential for ensuring that third-party partners are handling data securely and in compliance with privacy regulations.

Data Bias: Ensuring Fairness and Avoiding Discrimination

One of the most pressing challenges in AI-driven analytics is the issue of **data bias**, which occurs when the data used to train AI models contains inherent biases that lead to unfair or discriminatory outcomes. AI systems learn from historical data, and if that data reflects societal biases—whether related to race, gender, socioeconomic status, or other factors—then the AI models may perpetuate or even amplify these biases in their predictions or decisions.

For example, a hiring algorithm trained on historical data that reflects biased hiring practices may inadvertently favor candidates from certain demographics while discriminating against others. Similarly, a credit-scoring system might unfairly penalize individuals from marginalized communities if the underlying data includes biased financial information. The consequences of biased AI systems can be severe, leading to reputational damage, legal liability, and harm to individuals or groups who are unfairly treated by these systems.

To overcome the challenge of data bias, businesses must take proactive steps to ensure **fairness** and **transparency** in their AI systems. This begins with understanding the sources of bias in the data. Bias can enter at several stages, including during data collection, labeling, and processing. For instance, if a dataset is not representative of the population it is meant to serve (e.g., if it over-represents certain groups and under-represents others), then the AI model will produce skewed results. Therefore, businesses must prioritize **data diversity** and ensure that datasets are balanced and representative of different demographics and scenarios.

Additionally, **bias detection tools** can be used to evaluate AI models for fairness. These tools analyze model outputs to identify whether certain groups are being systematically disadvantaged. Once biases are detected, businesses can adjust their models by re-weighting the data or incorporating fairness constraints into the algorithms. For example, a hiring algorithm could be adjusted to ensure that it evaluates candidates based on skills and qualifications rather than demographic characteristics.

Transparency is also critical in mitigating bias. Businesses must be able to explain how their AI models work and the factors influencing the decisions they make. This is especially important in highly regulated industries like finance, healthcare, and criminal justice, where decisions can have life-altering consequences. Implementing **explainable AI (XAI)** frameworks ensures that AI models provide clear, understandable explanations for their predictions and decisions, enabling stakeholders to scrutinize the results for fairness and correctness.

Finally, fostering a **culture of ethical AI development** is essential for long-term success. This involves educating data scientists, developers, and business leaders about the potential for bias in AI and encouraging a commitment to developing equitable and inclusive AI systems. Engaging diverse teams in the design and development of AI solutions can also help surface potential biases that might otherwise go unnoticed.

Conclusion: Building Trust through Responsible Data Management

Overcoming the challenges of data privacy, security, and bias is crucial for businesses seeking to harness the power of AI and big data. As regulations evolve and customers become more aware of how their data is used, companies must prioritize responsible data management practices. By implementing robust privacy protections, ensuring strong data security, and addressing biases in AI systems, businesses can build trust with their stakeholders while maximizing the value of their data-driven insights.

Addressing these challenges requires a combination of technical solutions, such as encryption, bias detection, and explainable AI, as well as organizational strategies, including privacy-by-design, cybersecurity training, and promoting fairness in AI development. As businesses continue to rely on data and AI for decision-making, those that prioritize ethical data practices will be better positioned to thrive in an increasingly regulated and data-conscious world.

Chapter 3: AI-Powered Decision Models: Frameworks and Methodologies

- 3.1 Machine Learning and Deep Learning for Decision Making
- 3.2 Building AI Decision Models: A Step-by-Step Guide
- 3.3 Integrating AI with Existing Business Systems
- 3.4 Testing and Validating AI Decision Models
- 3.5 Continuous Improvement: Optimizing AI Models for Accuracy

Chapter 3: AI-Powered Decision Models: Frameworks and Methodologies

Chapter 3 delves into the core frameworks and methodologies that underpin AI-powered decision models. As businesses increasingly rely on AI to guide decision-making, understanding how to build and implement effective AI models becomes crucial. This chapter explores the processes and strategies that allow organizations to integrate AI into their decision-making frameworks, enhancing accuracy, efficiency, and strategic outcomes.

The chapter begins by examining **machine learning (ML)** and **deep learning**, which are the foundational technologies driving AI decision models. Machine learning enables systems to learn from data, identifying patterns and trends that humans might overlook. Deep learning, a subset of machine learning, mimics the human brain's neural networks to solve complex problems, making it especially effective in areas like image recognition, natural language processing, and advanced analytics. The section highlights how these technologies are applied to create predictive models that aid decision-making across industries.

Next, the chapter provides a **step-by-step guide** to building AI decision models. From data collection and preprocessing to training algorithms and validating results, this process outlines the critical stages necessary to ensure model reliability. Emphasis is placed on the importance of clean data, algorithm selection, and continuous evaluation to refine and optimize the decision models.

The chapter also discusses the integration of AI with **existing business systems**, ensuring that AI-driven models seamlessly complement traditional decision-making processes. Through practical examples, this section illustrates how businesses can align AI with their operational goals, improving decision quality without disrupting workflows.

Finally, the chapter covers **continuous improvement** and the need for constant model optimization. As business environments and data sources evolve, AI models must adapt to ensure sustained accuracy and relevance. This iterative approach allows businesses to maintain a competitive edge by continuously refining their decision-making frameworks.

Introduction

Artificial intelligence (AI) has revolutionized decision-making in businesses, offering powerful models that can process vast amounts of data, identify patterns, and generate predictions with greater speed and accuracy than traditional methods. AI-powered decision models leverage advanced algorithms, machine learning, and statistical techniques to provide organizations with actionable insights, allowing them to make data-driven choices that optimize efficiency, reduce risks, and increase profitability. This chapter delves into the various frameworks and methodologies that underpin AI-driven decision-making, from supervised and unsupervised learning models to reinforcement learning and deep learning techniques. By understanding these models, businesses can implement the appropriate AI tools to meet specific objectives, whether for automating processes, predicting market trends, or personalizing customer experiences.

3.1 Introduction to AI-Powered Decision Models

AI-powered decision models refer to algorithms and statistical methods used to guide decision-making in business environments. These models are trained on data to identify relationships between variables, predict outcomes, and recommend actions based on the identified patterns. Unlike traditional decision models, which rely on static rules and predefined inputs, AI-powered models continuously learn and improve their performance over time.

AI decision models can be categorized into several types, including:

- **Supervised learning models**, which are trained on labeled datasets and used for tasks like classification and regression.

- **Unsupervised learning models**, which identify hidden patterns in data without labeled outcomes, making them useful for clustering and anomaly detection.

- **Reinforcement learning models**, where agents learn to make decisions by receiving feedback through rewards or penalties.

- **Deep learning models**, which involve multi-layered neural networks capable of solving complex problems, such as image recognition and natural language processing.

Each of these methodologies offers unique advantages and is suited to different types of decision-making scenarios. In the following sections, we'll explore these models in detail, highlighting their key features, applications, and implementation considerations.

3.2 Supervised Learning for Decision Making

Supervised learning is one of the most widely used AI methodologies in business decision-making. In supervised learning, the model is trained on a dataset that includes both input variables (features) and the corresponding output variables (labels). The model learns to map the relationship between the inputs and outputs and can then predict future outcomes for new data points. Supervised learning is commonly used for **classification** tasks (where the goal is to categorize data into predefined classes) and **regression** tasks (where the goal is to predict continuous values).

Key Supervised Learning Models

1. **Linear Regression**: One of the simplest supervised learning algorithms, linear regression is used to model the relationship between a dependent variable and one or more independent variables. Businesses use linear regression to forecast sales, predict customer lifetime value, or analyze trends over time.

2. **Decision Trees**: Decision trees are flowchart-like models that split data based on certain criteria to arrive at decisions. They are intuitive and easy to interpret, making them popular in scenarios where transparency in decision-making is important, such as credit scoring or medical diagnoses.

3. **Random Forest**: A more advanced version of decision trees, random forests use multiple trees to make predictions. By aggregating the results of many decision trees, random forests reduce the risk of overfitting and improve accuracy. Random forests are widely used in fraud detection, customer segmentation, and risk assessment.

4. **Support Vector Machines (SVM)**: SVMs are powerful classifiers that separate data points into different classes by finding the optimal boundary (or hyperplane) between them. Businesses use SVMs for tasks like image recognition, spam detection, and product recommendation.

5. **Neural Networks**: Basic neural networks are used for supervised learning tasks and consist of layers of interconnected nodes. They are highly effective in complex classification problems, such as facial recognition and sentiment analysis.

Applications of Supervised Learning in Business

- **Customer Segmentation**: Supervised learning models can analyze customer data to identify key segments, allowing businesses to target their marketing efforts more effectively.

- **Churn Prediction**: AI models can predict the likelihood of a customer leaving the business, enabling proactive retention strategies.

- **Product Recommendation**: E-commerce platforms use supervised learning to recommend products to customers based on their browsing and purchasing history.

3.3 Unsupervised Learning for Pattern Discovery

Unsupervised learning differs from supervised learning in that it operates without labeled output data. Instead, the model is tasked with finding hidden patterns, structures, or relationships in the data. Unsupervised learning is useful for exploratory data analysis, where businesses want to uncover insights without knowing in advance what they are looking for.

Key Unsupervised Learning Models

1. **Clustering Algorithms**: Clustering algorithms, such as **k-means** and **hierarchical clustering**, group similar data points together based on certain characteristics. Businesses use clustering to segment

customers, identify market trends, or optimize inventory.

2. **Principal Component Analysis (PCA)**: PCA is a dimensionality reduction technique used to simplify large datasets by transforming them into a smaller set of variables that retain most of the original information. This helps businesses reduce complexity and focus on the most important variables in decision-making.

3. **Anomaly Detection**: AI models can detect unusual or outlying data points in a dataset, making them valuable for fraud detection, network security, and predictive maintenance in manufacturing.

Applications of Unsupervised Learning in Business

- **Market Segmentation**: Unsupervised learning helps identify distinct customer groups based on purchasing behavior, demographics, or online interactions, which can inform targeted marketing campaigns.

- **Anomaly Detection in Finance**: Banks and financial institutions use unsupervised models to detect fraudulent transactions or identify suspicious patterns in account activities.

- **Inventory Optimization**: By analyzing purchase and demand patterns, unsupervised learning models can help businesses optimize inventory levels and reduce storage costs.

3.4 Reinforcement Learning: Decision Making through Trial and Error

Reinforcement learning (RL) is a type of machine learning where an agent learns to make decisions by interacting with an environment and receiving feedback in the form of rewards or penalties. Unlike supervised and unsupervised learning, which rely on historical data, reinforcement learning involves dynamic decision-making, where the agent must continuously adjust its actions to maximize rewards over time. This makes RL particularly well-suited for real-time decision-making tasks.

Key Features of Reinforcement Learning

1. **Exploration vs. Exploitation**: In reinforcement learning, the agent must balance between exploring new strategies (exploration) and exploiting known strategies that have yielded rewards in the past

(exploitation). The challenge lies in finding the optimal balance to maximize long-term success.

2. **Policy and Value Functions**: Reinforcement learning uses **policy functions** to determine which action to take in a given situation and **value functions** to estimate the expected rewards for different actions. These functions evolve over time as the agent learns from its experiences.

3. **Markov Decision Processes (MDPs)**: Many reinforcement learning problems are modeled as MDPs, where the agent's decisions influence both the immediate rewards and the future state of the environment. MDPs provide a framework for understanding how actions taken today can affect long-term outcomes.

Applications of Reinforcement Learning in Business

- **Dynamic Pricing**: Online retailers can use reinforcement learning to dynamically adjust prices based on customer behavior, inventory levels, and competitor pricing.

- **Supply Chain Optimization**: RL models can help optimize supply chain operations by learning from past performance and adjusting strategies in real time to minimize costs and maximize efficiency.

- **Robotics and Automation**: Reinforcement learning is used in robotics to teach machines how to perform tasks autonomously, such as warehouse picking, product packaging, or autonomous driving.

3.5 Deep Learning for Complex Decision Making

Deep learning is a subset of machine learning that uses neural networks with multiple layers (hence the term "deep") to solve complex problems. Deep learning models can process unstructured data such as images, video, text, and speech, making them highly versatile for decision-making in various business contexts.

Key Deep Learning Models

1. **Convolutional Neural Networks (CNNs)**: CNNs are commonly used for image processing and recognition tasks, such as facial recognition, product visual search, or defect detection in manufacturing.

2. **Recurrent Neural Networks (RNNs)**: RNNs are designed for sequential data and are commonly used

for time-series forecasting, natural language processing (NLP), and speech recognition.

3. **Generative Adversarial Networks (GANs)**: GANs are used to generate new data samples, such as realistic images or text, and have applications in areas like design, media, and marketing.

Applications of Deep Learning in Business

- **Customer Service Automation**: Deep learning models, such as **chatbots** and **virtual assistants**, can handle customer queries in real-time, improving response times and reducing costs for businesses.

- **Demand Forecasting**: Retailers and manufacturers use deep learning to predict future demand, helping them adjust production schedules and manage inventory more effectively.

- **Product Design**: Businesses in the fashion or automotive industries use deep learning to create and visualize new product designs based on consumer preferences and market trends.

3.6 Frameworks for Implementing AI-Powered Decision Models

Building and implementing AI-powered decision models requires the right tools, frameworks, and platforms. Several frameworks make it easier for businesses to develop, train, and deploy AI models in decision-making processes:

1. **TensorFlow**: Developed by Google, TensorFlow is an open-source machine learning framework widely used for deep learning models. Its flexibility and scalability make it ideal for building complex AI-powered decision models.

2. **PyTorch**: PyTorch, developed by Facebook, is another popular deep learning framework that provides a more intuitive interface for developers, especially in the research and prototyping phases.

3.1 Machine Learning and Deep Learning for Decision Making

Machine learning (ML) and deep learning (DL) have transformed how businesses approach decision-making. These technologies enable companies to extract actionable insights from vast datasets, predict future trends, automate processes, and optimize decision-making. At their core, ML and DL models learn from data, enabling them to make informed decisions or predictions without the need for explicit programming.

Machine learning, as a subset of AI, includes various algorithms that learn from historical data to recognize patterns and make decisions. Deep learning, a specialized branch of machine learning, utilizes neural networks with many layers (hence the term "deep") to model complex data structures and solve problems involving unstructured data such as images, text, or audio. Both ML and DL are essential for developing AI-powered decision models that can adapt and evolve as new data becomes available.

Machine Learning for Decision Making

Machine learning models can be categorized into three types: **supervised learning**, **unsupervised learning**, and **reinforcement learning**. Each of these approaches serves distinct business needs and decision-making scenarios:

1. **Supervised Learning**: Supervised learning involves training a model on a labeled dataset, where the inputs (features) are linked to known outputs (labels). The model learns the relationship between inputs and outputs and applies this

knowledge to make predictions for new, unseen data. Supervised learning is commonly used in applications like fraud detection, customer churn prediction, and personalized marketing recommendations.

- o **Use Case**: A company can use supervised learning to forecast demand for products based on historical sales data, weather conditions, and marketing efforts, enabling better inventory management and resource allocation.

2. **Unsupervised Learning**: In contrast to supervised learning, unsupervised learning deals with unlabeled data. The model's objective is to discover hidden patterns or structures within the data without predefined outputs. Unsupervised learning is frequently applied in clustering, market segmentation, and anomaly detection.

- o **Use Case**: A retail business can use unsupervised learning to identify distinct customer groups based on purchasing behavior, allowing for more targeted marketing campaigns and personalized offers.

3. **Reinforcement Learning**: This type of machine learning focuses on training agents to make decisions by interacting with an environment and learning from feedback (rewards or penalties). Reinforcement learning is ideal for dynamic decision-making processes where the optimal decision is not immediately clear.

   o **Use Case**: In the e-commerce space, reinforcement learning can be used to optimize dynamic pricing strategies, where algorithms adjust prices in real-time based on demand, inventory levels, and competitor pricing.

Benefits of Machine Learning for Decision Making

- **Predictive Capabilities**: Machine learning models excel at forecasting future trends and behaviors, enabling businesses to make proactive decisions.
- **Automation**: By automating routine decision-making processes, machine learning reduces the need for manual intervention, freeing up resources for more strategic tasks.
- **Continuous Learning**: As more data becomes available, machine learning models improve over

time, leading to more accurate and refined decisions.

Deep Learning for Decision Making

Deep learning, a subset of machine learning, is particularly effective for tasks that involve complex data structures, such as images, videos, audio, and natural language. The power of deep learning lies in its use of **artificial neural networks**—multi-layered structures that can model intricate relationships in the data. Each layer of the network processes information at a different level of abstraction, allowing deep learning models to solve problems that are beyond the scope of traditional machine learning.

Key types of deep learning models include:

1. **Convolutional Neural Networks (CNNs)**: Primarily used for tasks related to image processing, CNNs are designed to automatically capture spatial hierarchies in images. CNNs are extensively used in industries such as healthcare for medical image analysis, retail for product recognition, and automotive for autonomous driving.

- Use Case: A retail company could use a CNN-based model to develop a visual search engine where customers upload images of products they want, and the system recommends similar items from the inventory.

2. **Recurrent Neural Networks (RNNs)**: RNNs are ideal for sequential data, such as time series data or natural language. RNNs retain information from previous inputs, allowing them to predict the next element in a sequence or generate coherent text based on prior context.

- Use Case: Financial institutions can use RNNs for stock market forecasting or to analyze trends in time-series data such as sales forecasts and demand planning.

3. **Generative Adversarial Networks (GANs)**: GANs consist of two neural networks, a generator and a discriminator, that work together to create new data samples. GANs are widely used in fields such as marketing for generating creative content, fashion for designing new products, and media for producing realistic-looking images or videos.

- o **Use Case**: A marketing team might use a GAN to create visually appealing promotional content or advertisements that align with a brand's style, reducing the time and cost associated with content creation.

Benefits of Deep Learning for Decision Making

- **Handling Unstructured Data**: Deep learning models are particularly effective in processing and analyzing unstructured data, such as customer reviews, social media posts, or product images, enabling businesses to derive insights that were previously inaccessible.
- **High Accuracy**: With sufficient data and computational resources, deep learning models can achieve exceptional accuracy in tasks such as image recognition, speech processing, and natural language understanding.
- **Adaptability**: Deep learning models can generalize well across different domains, making them versatile tools for solving a wide range of business problems.

Combining Machine Learning and Deep Learning for Better Decision Making

Many businesses combine machine learning and deep learning techniques to create robust decision models that can address both structured and unstructured data. For example, a company may use machine learning algorithms to analyze structured data, such as customer demographics and purchasing history, while using deep learning models to process unstructured data, such as product images or user-generated content. This hybrid approach enables more holistic decision-making, ensuring that businesses capitalize on all available data to make the best possible choices.

In conclusion, the integration of machine learning and deep learning into business decision-making processes allows organizations to tap into powerful tools for automation, prediction, and optimization. These AI-powered models not only streamline operations but also open new avenues for innovation and competitive advantage, enabling businesses to stay agile in a rapidly evolving digital landscape.

3.2 Building AI Decision Models: A Step-by-Step Guide

Creating AI decision models is a structured process that involves several key steps, from understanding the business problem to deploying the model in a real-world environment. These models help businesses automate decision-making, generate accurate predictions, and uncover valuable insights from data. The process of building these models requires a combination of data science techniques, algorithmic design, and continuous evaluation to ensure that the model remains effective over time.

In this section, we'll break down the process of building AI-powered decision models into clear, actionable steps, providing a practical guide to their development and implementation.

Step 1: Define the Business Problem

The first step in building an AI decision model is to clearly define the business problem you are trying to solve. This step involves:

- **Identifying the decision-making challenge**: What specific decisions or predictions need to be automated or improved? This could range from predicting customer churn to optimizing pricing strategies.

- **Understanding the stakeholders**: Who will be using the model's predictions? Are these business executives, operational teams, or customers? Defining the end-user helps shape how the model is designed.

- **Outlining business goals**: What are the success metrics? This could include metrics like improved sales, reduced churn, higher customer satisfaction, or operational efficiency.

For example, a retail business may want to use AI to predict demand for products during peak seasons. The business problem here is inventory management: ensuring that there are enough products to meet demand without overstocking.

Step 2: Data Collection and Preparation

Once the business problem is defined, the next step is to collect and prepare the necessary data. High-quality data is the foundation of any AI model. This step involves:

- **Data sourcing**: Identify internal and external data sources. Internal data might include sales records, customer transaction histories, or operational logs. External data could come from social media, weather reports, or market trends.

- **Data cleaning**: Raw data often contains errors, duplicates, or missing values that must be cleaned to ensure accurate modeling. Data cleaning involves handling missing data, outliers, and inconsistencies.

- **Feature selection**: Determine which data features (attributes or variables) are relevant to the business problem. For instance, in predicting product demand, features might include historical sales data, marketing campaigns, and seasonal trends.

- **Data transformation**: Sometimes data needs to be transformed into a format that can be used by AI algorithms. This may involve normalizing values, encoding categorical variables, or creating new features from existing data.

Step 3: Select the Right AI Model

With the data ready, the next step is to select the appropriate AI model. The choice of model depends on the type of problem (e.g., classification, regression, clustering) and the nature of the data. AI models can be broadly categorized into machine learning and deep learning models.

- **Supervised learning models**: Used when the data is labeled and the task is to predict an outcome. Examples include:
    - o **Linear regression** for predicting continuous values (e.g., sales forecast).
    - o **Logistic regression** or **decision trees** for classification tasks (e.g., customer churn prediction).
    - o **Random forests** and **support vector machines (SVMs)** for more complex predictions.
- **Unsupervised learning models**: Applied to unlabeled data, focusing on pattern discovery. Examples include:
    - o **K-means clustering** for customer segmentation.
    - o **Principal component analysis (PCA)** for dimensionality reduction.
- **Deep learning models**: Ideal for more complex tasks, such as image or speech recognition. Examples include:

- ○ **Convolutional neural networks (CNNs)** for image-based tasks.
- ○ **Recurrent neural networks (RNNs)** for sequential data (e.g., time series forecasting).

Choosing the right model often involves testing multiple algorithms and comparing their performance.

Step 4: Model Training and Testing

Once the model is selected, it needs to be trained on historical data to learn patterns and relationships. Model training involves:

- **Splitting the data**: Data is typically divided into a training set (used to train the model) and a test set (used to evaluate its performance). A common practice is to allocate 70-80% of the data for training and the remainder for testing.
- **Training the model**: The AI algorithm is trained by feeding it the training data. The model adjusts its internal parameters to minimize prediction errors (e.g., using loss functions in machine learning).

- **Cross-validation**: To ensure that the model generalizes well to unseen data, cross-validation techniques (e.g., k-fold cross-validation) are used. This involves splitting the training data into multiple subsets, training the model on each subset, and averaging the results.

During training, the model learns to recognize patterns in the data, but care must be taken to avoid over fitting (where the model learns the training data too well but fails to generalize to new data).

Step 5: Model Evaluation and Optimization

After training, the model is evaluated on the test data to measure its performance. This step involves:

- **Evaluation metrics**: Depending on the problem, various metrics are used to assess the model's performance. Common metrics include:
  - **Accuracy**: The proportion of correct predictions (for classification problems).
  - **Mean Absolute Error (MAE)** or **Root Mean Squared Error (RMSE)**: Used to

measure prediction accuracy in regression tasks.

- o **Precision, recall, and F1 score**: For evaluating classification models, particularly in imbalanced datasets.
- **Model tuning**: If the model does not perform as expected, various techniques can be applied to improve it, such as:
  - o **Hyper parameter tuning**: Adjusting parameters like learning rate, number of trees in random forests, or layers in neural networks to optimize performance.
  - o **Regularization techniques**: These techniques (e.g., L1 and L2 regularization) help prevent over fitting by penalizing overly complex models.
- **Feature engineering**: Improving the model's performance may also involve creating new features or modifying existing ones to better represent the underlying patterns in the data.

Step 6: Model Deployment

Once the model performs well on test data, it is ready for deployment. Deployment involves integrating the model into the business's decision-making processes or operational systems. Key considerations include:

- **Automation**: Integrate the model into a decision-making pipeline where it automatically analyzes data and generates predictions. For example, an e-commerce website may automatically adjust product recommendations based on the model's output.

- **Real-time vs. batch processing**: Determine whether the model will make real-time predictions (e.g., for fraud detection) or analyze data in batches (e.g., for monthly sales forecasting).

- **Model monitoring**: After deployment, the model's performance should be monitored regularly to ensure it continues to provide accurate results. This includes setting up alerts for performance degradation or significant changes in data patterns (e.g., concept drift).

Step 7: Continuous Improvement and Retraining

AI models are not static; they need to be updated as new data becomes available. Businesses should regularly retrain their models to reflect changes in the data and decision-making environment. Continuous improvement involves:

- **Monitoring performance**: Continuously track the model's accuracy and decision quality over time. If performance degrades, it may signal the need for retraining.
- **Data updates**: As new data is collected, feed it into the model to ensure it remains current and relevant.
- **Retraining frequency**: Depending on the application, models may need to be retrained daily, weekly, or monthly to maintain optimal performance.

For example, a recommendation system might need to be updated frequently to account for changes in customer preferences, while a demand forecasting model could be retrained quarterly based on new sales data. Building AI-powered decision models is a complex but rewarding process. By following a structured approach—starting with problem definition, moving through data collection and model selection, and finishing with evaluation and deployment—businesses can leverage AI to enhance their decision-making processes. Moreover, continuous monitoring and retraining are essential to ensuring that models remain effective as business conditions and data evolve. By investing in AI decision models, companies can gain a competitive edge, optimize their operations, and make smarter, data-driven decisions.

3.3 Integrating AI with Existing Business Systems

Integrating artificial intelligence (AI) with existing business systems is a crucial step for organizations aiming to leverage AI-driven insights and automation while ensuring continuity and efficiency in their operations. Successful integration not only enhances the functionality of existing systems but also enables businesses to maximize the value derived from their AI investments. This section provides a comprehensive guide on how to effectively integrate AI with existing business systems.

3.3.1 Understanding Integration Requirements

Before integrating AI with existing systems, it is essential to understand the specific requirements and objectives of the integration. This involves:

- **Assessing Business Needs**: Identify the key areas where AI can add value, such as automating routine tasks, improving decision-making, or enhancing customer experiences. For example, integrating AI into customer service systems might involve using chatbots to handle common inquiries and freeing up human agents for more complex issues.

- **Evaluating Existing Systems**: Review the current technology stack, including software applications, databases, and infrastructure. Determine how these systems interact with each other and identify any potential challenges in integrating AI technologies.

- **Defining Integration Goals**: Clearly outline the goals of the integration, such as improving operational efficiency, reducing manual effort, or providing better insights for decision-making. Set specific, measurable objectives to guide the integration process.

3.3.2 Selecting the Right AI Technology

Choosing the appropriate AI technology for integration depends on the business needs and existing systems. Key considerations include:

- **Type of AI Model**: Depending on the use case, select the right AI model or technology. For instance, if the goal is to enhance customer support, consider integrating natural language processing (NLP) models or chatbots. For predictive analytics, machine learning models that handle time-series data may be more appropriate.

- **Compatibility**: Ensure that the chosen AI technology is compatible with existing systems. This includes checking for integration capabilities, APIs, and data formats. Many modern AI solutions offer APIs or software development kits (SDKs) that facilitate integration with other systems.

- **Scalability**: Consider the scalability of the AI technology to accommodate future growth and increasing data volumes. Opt for solutions that can scale with your business needs and integrate seamlessly with other components of your technology stack.

3.3.3 Data Integration and Management

Data is the backbone of AI, and integrating AI with existing systems requires effective data management. This involves:

- **Data Integration**: Establish data pipelines to ensure that data flows seamlessly between AI systems and existing business applications. This may involve setting up ETL (extract, transform, load) processes to clean and transfer data between systems.

- **Data Quality**: Ensure data quality by addressing issues such as data inconsistencies, duplicates, and missing values. High-quality data is essential for training accurate AI models and making reliable predictions.

- **Data Security and Privacy**: Implement robust data security measures to protect sensitive information. Ensure compliance with relevant regulations and standards, such as GDPR or CCPA, when handling personal or confidential data.

- **Data Governance**: Establish data governance practices to manage data access, quality, and usage. Define roles and responsibilities for data management to ensure that data is used effectively and responsibly.

3.3.4 System Integration and Workflow Automation

Integrating AI with existing systems often involves modifying workflows and processes to leverage AI capabilities effectively. Key steps include:

- **Integration Architecture**: Design the integration architecture to connect AI systems with existing applications and infrastructure. This may involve using middleware, APIs, or integration platforms to facilitate communication between systems.

- **Workflow Mapping**: Map out existing workflows and identify areas where AI can enhance or automate processes. For example, integrating AI with a customer relationship management (CRM) system might involve automating lead scoring or personalizing customer interactions based on AI-generated insights.

- **Testing and Validation**: Conduct thorough testing to ensure that AI integrations function as expected and do not disrupt existing operations. Validate that the AI models provide accurate and actionable insights in real-world scenarios.

- **Change Management**: Implement change management practices to ensure a smooth transition to new AI-driven workflows. Communicate changes to stakeholders, provide training on new processes, and address any concerns or resistance to change.

3.3.5 Monitoring and Optimization

After integrating AI with existing systems, ongoing monitoring and optimization are essential to ensure continued success and improvement. This involves:

- **Performance Monitoring**: Continuously monitor the performance of AI systems to ensure they meet predefined objectives. Track key performance indicators (KPIs) and metrics related to the AI integration, such as accuracy, response time, and user satisfaction.

- **Feedback Loop**: Establish a feedback loop to gather input from users and stakeholders regarding the AI integration. Use this feedback to identify areas for improvement and make necessary adjustments.

- **Model Retraining**: Regularly update and retrain AI models to reflect changes in data and business conditions. Ensure that the models remain accurate and relevant as new data is collected and processed.

- **System Maintenance**: Perform routine maintenance and updates on both AI and existing systems to address any technical issues and ensure compatibility. Keep track of software updates, security patches, and performance enhancements.

3.3.6 Best Practices for AI Integration

To maximize the benefits of AI integration, consider the following best practices:

- **Start Small**: Begin with a pilot project or a limited scope to test the integration and validate its effectiveness before scaling it across the organization.

- **Collaborate with Stakeholders**: Involve key stakeholders from various departments in the integration process to ensure that the AI solution meets their needs and integrates smoothly with their workflows.

- **Document Processes**: Document the integration process, including system configurations, data flows, and any customizations made. This documentation will be valuable for troubleshooting, training, and future enhancements.

- **Focus on User Experience**: Ensure that the AI integration enhances the user experience by providing intuitive interfaces and actionable insights. User adoption is critical to the success of AI initiatives, so prioritize usability and accessibility.

- **Evaluate ROI**: Assess the return on investment (ROI) of the AI integration by comparing the benefits achieved with the costs incurred. Evaluate the impact on business objectives and determine if the integration delivers the expected value. Integrating AI with existing business systems requires careful planning, selection of appropriate technologies, effective data management, and continuous monitoring. By following a structured approach and adhering to best practices, organizations can successfully incorporate AI into their operations, driving innovation, efficiency, and improved decision-making. AI integration not only enhances the functionality of existing systems but also positions businesses to capitalize on new opportunities and stay competitive in an increasingly digital landscape.

3.4 Testing and Validating AI Decision Models

Testing and validating AI decision models are critical steps in ensuring that these models function correctly, provide reliable results, and meet the business objectives for which they were designed. This process involves rigorous evaluation to confirm that the models are not only accurate but also robust, scalable, and aligned with real-world scenarios. Effective testing and validation are essential to mitigate risks, optimize performance, and build trust in AI systems.

The Importance of Testing and Validation

AI models, while powerful, are susceptible to errors, biases, and performance degradation if not properly tested and validated. Rigorous testing ensures that the model performs as expected across various scenarios, handles edge cases, and maintains accuracy under different conditions. Validation helps confirm that the model's predictions or decisions align with the intended business outcomes and user requirements. Proper testing and validation can prevent costly mistakes, enhance user satisfaction, and support informed decision-making.

Key Phases of Testing and Validation

1. **Unit Testing**: The initial phase of testing involves unit testing, where individual components of the AI model are tested in isolation. This includes verifying the functionality of data preprocessing steps, feature engineering processes, and model

algorithms. Unit testing ensures that each component works correctly before integrating them into a complete system.

- o **Data Integrity Checks**: Verify that data preprocessing steps, such as normalization, encoding, and imputation, are correctly applied and do not introduce errors or inconsistencies.

- o **Algorithm Validation**: Ensure that the chosen algorithms perform as expected on sample data. This involves checking that the algorithms handle inputs and outputs correctly and produce valid results.

2. **Integration Testing**: After unit testing, integration testing examines how the AI model interacts with other components and systems within the broader application. This phase focuses on ensuring that the model integrates seamlessly with existing business processes and technologies.

- o **System Compatibility**: Test the integration of the AI model with other systems, such as databases, APIs, and user interfaces, to ensure smooth data flow and functionality.

o **Workflow Verification**: Validate that the AI model supports and enhances existing workflows. This includes checking that the model's predictions or decisions are correctly utilized in the decision-making process.

3. **Performance Testing**: Performance testing assesses how well the AI model performs under various conditions, including different data volumes and operational loads. This phase helps identify potential bottlenecks, scalability issues, and areas for optimization.

   o **Load Testing**: Evaluate the model's performance under high data volumes and stress conditions. Ensure that the model can handle large datasets and maintain acceptable response times.

   o **Scalability Assessment**: Test the model's ability to scale with increasing data and user demands. This involves checking that the model remains efficient and accurate as it processes larger or more complex datasets.

4. **Validation with Real-World Data**: Validating the AI model with real-world data is crucial to ensure

that it performs accurately in practical scenarios. This phase involves testing the model on data that closely resembles the data it will encounter in production.

- o **Real-World Testing**: Apply the model to live or near-live data to evaluate its performance in real-world conditions. Compare the model's predictions or decisions against actual outcomes to assess accuracy and reliability.

- o **Edge Case Evaluation**: Identify and test edge cases or unusual scenarios that may not be well-represented in training data. Ensure that the model can handle these cases without significant errors or biases.

5. **Bias and Fairness Testing**: Bias and fairness testing is essential to ensure that the AI model does not produce discriminatory or unfair outcomes. This phase involves evaluating the model's performance across different demographic groups and ensuring that it adheres to ethical standards.

- o **Bias Detection**: Analyze the model's predictions for potential biases based on attributes such as race, gender, age, or socioeconomic status. Use techniques such as fairness-aware algorithms or disparity analysis to detect and mitigate biases.

- o **Fairness Assessment**: Ensure that the model's decisions are fair and equitable. Evaluate the model's impact on different user groups and confirm that it adheres to ethical guidelines and regulatory requirements.

6. **User Acceptance Testing (UAT)**: User acceptance testing involves assessing the AI model's effectiveness from the perspective of end-users. This phase ensures that the model meets user needs, is intuitive to use, and delivers value.

- o **User Feedback**: Collect feedback from users who interact with the AI model. Assess their satisfaction with the model's performance, usability, and overall impact on their tasks.

- o **Iterative Improvement**: Use user feedback to identify areas for improvement and make necessary adjustments to the model. Iterative testing and refinement help align the model with user expectations and enhance its effectiveness.

Continuous Monitoring and Maintenance

Testing and validation are not one-time activities but ongoing processes. Once the AI model is deployed, continuous monitoring is essential to ensure that it maintains performance and accuracy over time. Key aspects of continuous monitoring include:

- **Performance Tracking**: Regularly monitor the model's performance metrics, such as accuracy, precision, and recall. Track changes in performance and address any degradation promptly.
- **Model Retraining**: Periodically retrain the model with new data to ensure that it remains current and adapts to changes in data patterns and business conditions.
- **Anomaly Detection**: Implement mechanisms to detect anomalies or unexpected behavior in the model's predictions. Address any issues that arise to maintain model reliability.

Testing and validating AI decision models are critical for ensuring their effectiveness, accuracy, and alignment with business objectives. By following a structured approach that includes unit testing, integration testing, performance testing, real-world validation, bias and fairness assessment, and user acceptance testing, organizations can build robust AI models that deliver valuable insights and drive informed decision-making. Continuous monitoring and maintenance further ensure that AI models remain effective and reliable as they are deployed in dynamic business environments.

3.5 Continuous Improvement: Optimizing AI Models for Accuracy

Continuous improvement is a cornerstone of effective AI model management, ensuring that models remain accurate, relevant, and valuable over time. AI models, like any other technology, can degrade in performance due to changes in data, evolving business needs, or shifts in external conditions. Therefore, ongoing optimization is essential to maintain and enhance the accuracy and effectiveness of AI models. This section outlines the strategies and practices for continuously improving AI models to achieve and sustain high accuracy.

The Need for Continuous Improvement

AI models are trained on historical data and may encounter shifts or changes in patterns over time, a phenomenon known as "concept drift." Additionally, new data or insights may reveal opportunities for refining models to better meet business objectives. Continuous improvement is necessary to adapt to these changes, ensure the model's predictions remain accurate, and optimize performance for evolving requirements.

Key Strategies for Continuous Improvement

1. **Monitoring Model Performance**
   o **Performance Metrics**: Continuously track performance metrics such as accuracy, precision, recall, F1 score, and AUC-ROC (Area Under the Receiver Operating Characteristic Curve). These metrics provide insights into how well the model is performing and where adjustments might be needed.
   o **Real-Time Monitoring**: Implement real-time monitoring systems to detect performance issues promptly. Automated

alerts can help identify when the model's accuracy drops below acceptable thresholds, allowing for immediate intervention.

2. **Data Quality Management**

   o **Data Drift Detection**: Monitor for data drift, which occurs when the statistical properties of the input data change over time. Techniques such as statistical tests or drift detection algorithms can help identify when data drift occurs, signaling the need for model retraining.

   o **Data Enrichment**: Regularly update and enrich the training dataset with new, relevant data to ensure that the model reflects current trends and patterns. Incorporating diverse data sources can improve model robustness and accuracy.

3. **Model Retraining and Updates**

   o **Retraining Schedule**: Establish a retraining schedule based on factors such as data volume, frequency of changes in data, and business requirements. Models may need to be retrained monthly, quarterly, or annually, depending on the application.

o **Incremental Learning**: For models that continuously receive new data, consider incremental learning techniques that allow the model to update its knowledge without retraining from scratch. This approach can be more efficient and responsive to changes.

4. **Feature Engineering and Selection**

   o **Feature Reassessment**: Periodically reassess the features used in the model. New features may become relevant, or existing features may become less important. Feature engineering techniques, such as creating new features or selecting the most impactful ones, can enhance model performance.

   o **Dimensionality Reduction**: Apply dimensionality reduction techniques, such as Principal Component Analysis (PCA) or feature selection algorithms, to eliminate irrelevant or redundant features that may negatively impact model accuracy.

5. **Hyper parameter Tuning**

   o **Optimization Techniques**: Use hyperparameter tuning methods to optimize model parameters for better performance.

Techniques such as grid search, random search, or Bayesian optimization can help find the optimal combination of hyperparameters.

- o **Automated Tuning**: Implement automated machine learning (AutoML) tools that can efficiently perform hyperparameter tuning and model selection, saving time and improving accuracy.

6. **Algorithmic Adjustments**

- o **Model Selection**: Evaluate and compare different algorithms or models to identify those that perform better with current data. Switching to a more advanced or suitable algorithm may improve accuracy.

- o **Ensemble Methods**: Consider using ensemble methods, such as boosting, bagging, or stacking, to combine multiple models and improve overall accuracy. Ensemble methods can enhance performance by leveraging the strengths of different models.

7. **User Feedback Integration**

o **Feedback Loops**: Establish feedback loops with end-users to gather insights on model performance and areas for improvement. User feedback can provide valuable information on how well the model meets their needs and where adjustments are necessary.

o **A/B Testing**: Conduct A/B testing to compare different versions of the model and evaluate their performance in real-world scenarios. This approach helps identify the most effective model configuration based on user interactions and outcomes.

8. **Ethical and Fairness Considerations**

o **Bias Monitoring**: Continuously monitor for biases in the model's predictions and ensure that the model's outputs are fair and unbiased. Regular audits and fairness assessments can help identify and address any discriminatory outcomes.

o **Ethical Guidelines**: Adhere to ethical guidelines and best practices for AI development. Ensure that the model aligns with ethical standards and regulatory requirements, and make necessary adjustments to maintain fairness and transparency.

9. **Documentation and Knowledge Sharing**

   o **Documentation**: Maintain comprehensive documentation of the model's development, testing, and improvement processes. This documentation serves as a reference for understanding the model's evolution and making informed decisions about updates.

   o **Knowledge Sharing**: Share insights and lessons learned from model improvements with the broader team. Collaborative knowledge sharing can help disseminate best practices and enhance the overall effectiveness of AI initiatives.

Continuous improvement is essential for optimizing AI models and ensuring their accuracy, relevance, and effectiveness. By implementing strategies such as performance monitoring, data quality management, model retraining, feature engineering, hyperparameter tuning, algorithmic adjustments, user feedback integration, and ethical considerations, organizations can maintain and enhance the value of their AI models over time. Embracing a culture of continuous improvement allows businesses to adapt to changes, stay competitive, and leverage AI to drive informed decision-making and achieve their strategic goals.

Chapter 4: Real-World Applications of AI in Business Strategy

- 4.1 AI in Marketing: Personalization and Customer Engagement
- 4.2 Supply Chain Optimization with AI
- 4.3 AI in Financial Services: Risk Management and Fraud Detection
- 4.4 Human Resources and Talent Management using AI
- 4.5 AI-Driven Innovation in Product Development

Chapter 4: Real-World Applications of AI in Business Strategy

Chapter 4 focuses on the tangible impact of AI in real-world business strategies, demonstrating how companies across industries are utilizing AI to optimize operations, enhance customer experiences, and drive innovation. Through case studies and practical examples, this chapter illustrates how AI is no longer just a theoretical tool but a transformative force reshaping business landscapes. The chapter begins by exploring **AI in marketing and customer engagement**, where AI technologies such as machine learning, predictive analytics, and natural language processing (NLP) are used to create personalized experiences. Businesses can analyze customer data to predict behavior, segment audiences, and deliver targeted content, resulting in higher engagement and improved customer satisfaction. AI also powers recommendation engines, chatbots, and sentiment analysis, which are increasingly integral to modern marketing strategies. Next, the chapter delves into **AI's role in supply chain optimization**. By leveraging AI for demand forecasting, inventory management, and logistics, companies can streamline operations, reduce costs, and improve efficiency. AI algorithms help predict supply chain disruptions, enabling proactive risk management and maintaining business continuity in the face of unexpected challenges. The chapter then shifts to **AI in financial services**, focusing on risk management and fraud detection. Financial institutions are using AI to analyze transaction data, identify fraudulent activities, and assess credit risks. AI models, particularly in fintech, offer faster, more accurate financial decisions while improving security measures. Another major focus is the use of **AI in human resources and talent management**. From screening resumes and conducting initial interviews to monitoring employee engagement and predicting turnover, AI plays a pivotal role in making HR processes more efficient and data-driven. Finally, the chapter covers **AI-driven product development and innovation**, where AI technologies assist companies in analyzing market trends, customer preferences, and competitive landscapes to innovate new products faster and more effectively. Chapter 4 provides a comprehensive overview of how AI is being applied across various business domains, showcasing its value as an indispensable tool for modern business strategy.

Introduction

Artificial Intelligence (AI) has transformed business strategy across various industries, offering innovative solutions to complex challenges and unlocking new opportunities for growth. This chapter explores the practical applications of AI in business strategy, highlighting how organizations leverage AI to drive efficiency, enhance decision-making, and gain a competitive edge. By examining real-world examples and case studies, this chapter illustrates the diverse ways AI can be applied to achieve strategic objectives.

4.1 AI in Customer Experience Enhancement

AI technologies have revolutionized customer experience management by enabling personalized interactions, efficient service, and deeper insights into customer behavior. Key applications include:

- **Chatbots and Virtual Assistants**: AI-powered chatbots and virtual assistants provide instant, 24/7 customer support, handling routine inquiries, processing transactions, and resolving issues. These tools enhance customer satisfaction by offering quick and accurate responses, freeing up human agents to handle more complex tasks. For example, companies like Sephora and H&M use chatbots to assist customers with product recommendations and order tracking.

- **Personalized Recommendations**: AI algorithms analyze customer data, such as purchase history, browsing behavior, and preferences, to deliver personalized product or content recommendations. Platforms like Amazon and Netflix use sophisticated recommendation engines to suggest relevant products or shows, increasing user engagement and sales.

- **Sentiment Analysis**: AI-driven sentiment analysis tools analyze customer feedback, reviews, and social media posts to gauge public opinion and identify areas for improvement. Businesses can use these insights to address customer concerns, enhance product offerings, and tailor marketing strategies.

4.2 AI in Supply Chain Optimization

AI has transformed supply chain management by enhancing efficiency, reducing costs, and improving decision-making. Key applications include:

- **Demand Forecasting**: AI models analyze historical sales data, market trends, and external factors to predict future demand. Accurate demand forecasting helps businesses optimize inventory levels, reduce stockouts or overstock situations, and improve supply chain planning. Companies like Walmart and Procter & Gamble use AI for advanced demand forecasting.

- **Supply Chain Visibility**: AI-powered platforms provide real-time visibility into supply chain operations, tracking shipments, monitoring supplier performance, and identifying potential disruptions. This visibility enables businesses to respond proactively to issues, such as delays or shortages, and make informed decisions.

- **Route Optimization**: AI algorithms optimize delivery routes based on factors like traffic conditions, weather, and customer locations. This optimization reduces transportation costs, improves delivery times, and enhances overall supply chain efficiency. Companies like UPS and FedEx use AI for route planning and logistics optimization.

4.3 AI in Financial Services

In the financial services industry, AI has revolutionized various aspects of operations, from risk management to customer service. Key applications include:

- **Fraud Detection**: AI models analyze transaction patterns and detect anomalies that may indicate fraudulent activity. Machine learning algorithms continuously learn from new data to identify evolving fraud schemes and reduce false positives. Financial institutions like JPMorgan Chase and Mastercard use AI for fraud detection and prevention.

- **Algorithmic Trading**: AI-driven algorithms execute trades at high speeds based on market data and predefined strategies. These algorithms can analyze vast amounts of data in real time, making trading decisions faster and more accurately than human traders. Firms like Renaissance Technologies and Citadel use AI for algorithmic trading.

- **Credit Scoring**: AI models assess creditworthiness by analyzing a wide range of data, including financial history, transaction behavior, and alternative data sources. This approach provides more accurate credit scoring and reduces the risk of defaults. Companies like Zest AI and Upstart use AI for credit scoring and underwriting.

4.4 AI in Marketing and Advertising

AI has transformed marketing and advertising by enabling targeted campaigns, optimizing ad spend, and improving customer engagement. Key applications include:

- **Programmatic Advertising**: AI algorithms automate the buying and placement of digital ads, targeting specific audiences based on data such as browsing behavior, demographics, and interests. This automation improves ad relevance and efficiency, leading to higher ROI. Companies like Google and Facebook use AI for programmatic advertising.

- **Content Creation**: AI tools generate content, such as product descriptions, social media posts, and marketing copy, based on data-driven insights. Natural language generation (NLG) algorithms create human-like text that aligns with brand messaging and engages audiences. Platforms like Copy.ai and Jasper use AI for content creation.

- **Customer Segmentation**: AI models analyze customer data to identify distinct segments with similar behaviors, preferences, and needs. This segmentation allows businesses to tailor marketing campaigns and offers to specific groups, increasing engagement and conversion rates.

4.5 AI in Human Resources and Talent Management

AI has reshaped human resources (HR) and talent management by streamlining processes, improving recruitment, and enhancing employee experience. Key applications include:

- **Recruitment and Talent Acquisition**: AI-powered tools automate candidate screening, resume parsing, and initial assessments, reducing the time and effort required to find qualified candidates. AI can also analyze candidate fit based on skills, experience, and cultural alignment. Companies like HireVue and Pymetrics use AI for recruitment and talent assessment.
- **Employee Engagement and Retention**: AI platforms analyze employee feedback, performance data, and engagement metrics to identify trends and

predict turnover risk. This analysis helps HR teams implement targeted strategies to enhance employee satisfaction and retention.

- **Training and Development**: AI-driven learning platforms offer personalized training and development programs based on employees' skills, career goals, and performance. These platforms use adaptive learning techniques to provide customized content and recommendations, improving employee growth and productivity.

4.6 AI in Healthcare and Life Sciences

AI has made significant advancements in healthcare and life sciences, improving patient care, accelerating research, and optimizing operations. Key applications include:

- **Medical Imaging**: AI algorithms analyze medical images, such as X-rays, MRIs, and CT scans, to assist radiologists in diagnosing conditions and identifying abnormalities. AI-powered imaging tools enhance diagnostic accuracy and speed up image analysis. Companies like Zebra Medical Vision and Aidoc use AI for medical imaging.

- **Drug Discovery**: AI models analyze vast amounts of biomedical data to identify potential drug candidates, predict drug interactions, and accelerate the drug discovery process. This approach reduces the time and cost of bringing new drugs to market. Firms like DeepMind and Insilico Medicine use AI for drug discovery and development.

- **Patient Monitoring and Management**: AI-powered systems monitor patient health data in real time, providing alerts and recommendations for personalized care. These systems can track vital signs, detect early signs of deterioration, and support remote patient management. Companies like IBM Watson Health and Medtronic use AI for patient monitoring and management.

AI has a profound impact on business strategy across diverse industries, offering innovative solutions to enhance customer experience, optimize supply chains, improve financial services, and drive marketing and HR initiatives. By leveraging AI technologies, organizations can achieve greater efficiency, make data-driven decisions, and gain a competitive edge in the marketplace. The real-world applications highlighted in this chapter demonstrate the transformative potential of AI and underscore its importance in shaping the future of business strategy. As AI continues to evolve, its role in business strategy will expand, presenting new opportunities and challenges for organizations to navigate.

4.1 AI in Marketing: Personalization and Customer Engagement

Artificial Intelligence (AI) has revolutionized marketing by enabling unprecedented levels of personalization and enhancing customer engagement. AI-driven technologies allow businesses to tailor their marketing strategies to individual preferences, optimize customer interactions, and drive higher levels of engagement and conversion. This section explores the key applications of AI in marketing, highlighting how these technologies are reshaping customer experiences and influencing marketing outcomes.

Personalized Marketing Campaigns

AI has transformed the way businesses create and execute marketing campaigns by enabling highly personalized content and offers. This personalization is achieved through advanced data analysis, machine learning algorithms, and real-time insights.

172

- **Targeted Content Delivery**: AI algorithms analyze customer data, including browsing history, purchase behavior, and demographic information, to deliver tailored content and recommendations. For example, e-commerce platforms like Amazon use AI to suggest products based on users' past purchases and browsing patterns, resulting in more relevant and engaging content for each customer.

- **Dynamic Pricing**: AI-driven dynamic pricing models adjust prices in real-time based on factors such as demand, competition, and customer behavior. This approach allows businesses to optimize pricing strategies, maximize revenue, and offer personalized discounts or promotions to individual customers. Companies like Uber and airlines use dynamic pricing to adjust fares and ticket prices according to market conditions and customer profiles.

- **Email Marketing Optimization**: AI tools enhance email marketing by personalizing subject lines, content, and send times based on individual recipient preferences and behavior. Machine learning models can analyze open rates, click-through rates, and user interactions to optimize email campaigns and improve engagement. Platforms like Mailchimp and SendGrid offer AI-powered email marketing solutions that help businesses achieve better results.

Enhanced Customer Segmentation

AI enables more granular and accurate customer segmentation by analyzing large volumes of data to identify distinct customer groups with similar behaviors and preferences.

- **Behavioral Segmentation**: AI models analyze customer interactions, such as website visits, social media activity, and purchase history, to segment customers based on their behavior. This segmentation allows businesses to target specific groups with tailored messages and offers, increasing the relevance of marketing efforts. For instance, Spotify uses AI to segment users based on listening habits and provide personalized playlists and recommendations.
- **Predictive Analytics**: AI-powered predictive analytics forecast future customer behavior and preferences based on historical data. By identifying

patterns and trends, businesses can anticipate customer needs, personalize marketing strategies, and enhance customer experiences. For example, retailers use predictive analytics to forecast purchasing behavior and tailor marketing campaigns to seasonal trends and individual preferences.

- **Customer Lifetime Value (CLV) Prediction**: AI models predict the potential value of customers over their lifetime by analyzing factors such as purchasing frequency, average order value, and retention rates. This prediction helps businesses allocate resources effectively, prioritize high-value customers, and design targeted retention strategies. Companies like Salesforce and HubSpot offer AI-driven CLV prediction tools to optimize customer relationship management.

Real-Time Customer Interaction

AI facilitates real-time interactions with customers through chatbots, virtual assistants, and other automated tools, improving responsiveness and engagement.

- **Chatbots and Virtual Assistants**: AI-powered chatbots and virtual assistants provide instant support and personalized interactions with customers. These tools handle routine inquiries, assist with product recommendations, and guide users through the purchasing process. For example, companies like Sephora and H&M use chatbots to enhance customer service and streamline the shopping experience.

- **Sentiment Analysis**: AI-driven sentiment analysis tools analyze customer feedback, reviews, and social media posts to gauge customer sentiment and identify emerging trends. This analysis helps businesses understand customer opinions, address concerns, and tailor marketing messages to align with customer expectations. Platforms like Brandwatch and Lexalytics offer AI-based sentiment analysis solutions for brands.

- **Social Media Engagement**: AI algorithms analyze social media interactions to identify influencers, track brand mentions, and assess engagement levels. Businesses can use these insights to optimize social media strategies, engage with followers, and respond to customer feedback in real-time. Tools like Sprout Social and Hootsuite provide AI-powered social media analytics and engagement solutions.

Content Generation and Optimization

AI enhances content creation and optimization by generating high-quality content, analyzing its effectiveness, and optimizing it for better performance.

- **Content Creation**: AI-driven content generation tools use natural language processing (NLP) to create human-like text for various purposes, such as blog posts, product descriptions, and marketing copy. These tools help businesses produce engaging content at scale, saving time and resources. Companies like Copy.ai and Jasper offer AI-powered content creation solutions.

- **SEO Optimization**: AI algorithms analyze search engine trends, keyword performance, and competitor strategies to optimize content for search engines. By providing recommendations for keyword usage, content structure, and on-page SEO, AI helps businesses improve their search engine rankings and drive organic traffic. Platforms like Clearscope and SEMrush use AI to enhance SEO efforts.

- **A/B Testing and Optimization**: AI tools automate A/B testing by analyzing performance data from different versions of marketing materials, such as landing pages or ad creatives. This analysis helps businesses identify the most effective variations and optimize their marketing strategies for better results. Tools like Optimizely and Adobe Target offer AI-powered A/B testing and optimization solutions.

Ethical Considerations and Privacy

As AI becomes more integrated into marketing strategies, businesses must address ethical considerations and privacy concerns related to data collection and usage.

- **Data Privacy**: AI-driven personalization relies on collecting and analyzing large amounts of customer data. Businesses must ensure compliance with data privacy regulations, such as GDPR and CCPA, and implement robust data protection measures to safeguard customer information.
- **Transparency and Consent**: Businesses should be transparent about their data collection practices and

obtain explicit consent from customers for data usage. Providing clear information about how data will be used and offering options for opting out can build trust and enhance customer relationships.

- **Bias and Fairness**: AI models can inadvertently introduce biases based on the data they are trained on. Businesses must regularly evaluate and mitigate biases in AI systems to ensure fair and equitable treatment of all customers.

AI has revolutionized marketing by enabling highly personalized experiences, optimizing customer interactions, and enhancing engagement. Through applications such as targeted content delivery, behavioral segmentation, real-time customer interaction, content generation, and SEO optimization, AI empowers businesses to create more effective and relevant marketing strategies. However, it is essential to address ethical considerations and privacy concerns to ensure responsible and transparent use of AI technologies. By leveraging AI's capabilities and adhering to ethical practices, businesses can drive meaningful customer experiences and achieve their marketing objectives in an increasingly competitive landscape.

4.2 Supply Chain Optimization with AI

AI has become a game-changer in supply chain management, offering solutions that enhance efficiency, reduce costs, and improve decision-making. By leveraging AI technologies, businesses can optimize various aspects of their supply chains, from demand forecasting to logistics management. This section explores how AI is transforming supply chain operations and the benefits it brings to organizations.

Demand Forecasting

Accurate demand forecasting is crucial for effective supply chain management. AI-powered tools analyze historical data, market trends, and external factors to predict future demand with greater precision.

- **Predictive Analytics**: AI algorithms utilize historical sales data, seasonality, and market trends to forecast demand. By identifying patterns and trends, businesses can anticipate future needs and adjust inventory levels accordingly. For example, retail giants like Walmart and Target use AI for predictive analytics to optimize inventory and reduce stockouts.

- **Machine Learning Models**: Machine learning models continuously learn from new data to improve forecasting accuracy over time. These models can adapt to changing market conditions and adjust predictions based on real-time information. Companies like Amazon use machine learning for dynamic demand forecasting, ensuring optimal stock levels and efficient operations.

- **External Factors Analysis**: AI systems incorporate external factors such as weather conditions, economic indicators, and social trends into demand forecasts. This comprehensive analysis helps businesses account for variables that may impact demand, leading to more accurate predictions and better supply chain planning.

Supply Chain Visibility

AI enhances supply chain visibility by providing real-time insights into various aspects of operations, from inventory levels to shipment statuses.

- **Real-Time Tracking**: AI-powered platforms track shipments, monitor inventory levels, and provide real-time updates on supply chain activities. This

181

visibility allows businesses to proactively address issues such as delays or disruptions and make informed decisions. Companies like Maersk and DHL use AI for real-time supply chain tracking and management.

- **Predictive Maintenance**: AI algorithms predict equipment failures and maintenance needs based on historical data and real-time sensor information. By anticipating maintenance requirements, businesses can prevent unplanned downtime and ensure smooth operations. Manufacturing firms like General Electric use AI for predictive maintenance in their supply chains.

- **Supplier Performance Monitoring**: AI tools analyze supplier performance data, including delivery times, quality metrics, and compliance records, to assess and manage supplier relationships. This monitoring helps businesses identify reliable suppliers, negotiate better terms, and mitigate risks. Platforms like Ariba and Jaggaer offer AI-driven supplier performance management solutions.

Route Optimization

AI improves logistics efficiency by optimizing delivery routes and reducing transportation costs. Key applications include:

- **Dynamic Routing**: AI algorithms analyze factors such as traffic conditions, weather, and delivery schedules to determine the most efficient routes for transportation. Dynamic routing minimizes travel time, reduces fuel consumption, and improves delivery accuracy. Companies like UPS and FedEx use AI for route optimization in their logistics operations.

- **Load Optimization**: AI tools optimize cargo loading by calculating the most efficient way to arrange goods in transportation vehicles. This optimization maximizes space utilization, reduces transportation costs, and minimizes environmental impact. Solutions like the ones offered by Locus and Project44 leverage AI for load optimization and logistics management.

- **Supply Chain Network Design**: AI algorithms help businesses design and optimize their supply chain networks by analyzing factors such as facility locations, transportation routes, and inventory levels. This design ensures an efficient and cost-effective supply chain structure. Companies like IBM and Oracle provide AI-powered supply chain network optimization tools.

Inventory Management

AI enhances inventory management by optimizing stock levels, reducing carrying costs, and minimizing stockouts.

- **Automated Replenishment**: AI systems automate inventory replenishment by analyzing sales data, lead times, and supplier performance. Automated replenishment ensures that stock levels are maintained at optimal levels, reducing the risk of stockouts and overstock situations. Retailers like Zara and Costco use AI for automated inventory management.

- **Inventory Optimization**: AI algorithms analyze historical data, demand patterns, and supplier lead times to optimize inventory levels across different locations. This optimization helps businesses balance inventory costs with service levels, ensuring efficient stock management. Companies like Unilever and PepsiCo leverage AI for inventory optimization.

- **Demand-Driven Inventory**: AI-driven inventory management systems align stock levels with real-time demand signals. By integrating demand forecasts with inventory management, businesses can respond quickly to changes in demand and adjust inventory accordingly. Solutions from firms like Blue Yonder and E2open use AI for demand-driven inventory management.

Risk Management and Resilience

AI helps businesses identify and mitigate risks in their supply chains, improving resilience and continuity.

- **Risk Assessment**: AI models assess supply chain risks by analyzing factors such as supplier reliability, geopolitical events, and natural disasters. This assessment helps businesses identify potential vulnerabilities and develop risk mitigation strategies. Companies like Riskmethods and Everstream Analytics offer AI-driven risk management solutions.
- **Scenario Planning**: AI-powered scenario planning tools simulate various supply chain scenarios to assess the impact of potential disruptions. This

planning helps businesses prepare for unexpected events and develop contingency plans to maintain operations. Platforms like Kinaxis and Llamasoft provide AI-driven scenario planning and simulation capabilities.

- **Supply Chain Resilience**: AI enhances supply chain resilience by providing insights into alternative sourcing options, backup suppliers, and contingency plans. This resilience ensures that businesses can adapt to disruptions and maintain continuity in their supply chain operations.

Ethical Considerations and Challenges

As AI becomes integral to supply chain management, businesses must address ethical considerations and challenges related to data privacy, transparency, and bias.

- **Data Privacy**: AI-driven supply chain solutions rely on extensive data collection and analysis. Businesses must ensure that data privacy regulations are followed and implement measures to protect sensitive information. Compliance with regulations such as GDPR and CCPA is essential for maintaining customer trust.

- **Transparency**: Transparency in AI decision-making is crucial for building trust with stakeholders. Businesses should provide clear explanations of how AI algorithms make decisions and ensure that the decision-making process is understandable and accountable.

- **Bias and Fairness**: AI models can inadvertently introduce biases based on the data they are trained on. Businesses must regularly evaluate and address biases to ensure fair and equitable supply chain management. Ethical AI practices and ongoing audits can help mitigate potential biases.

AI has significantly transformed supply chain management by enhancing demand forecasting, improving supply chain visibility, optimizing routes, and refining inventory management. By leveraging AI technologies, businesses can achieve greater efficiency, reduce costs, and build resilient supply chains that adapt to changing conditions. Addressing ethical considerations and challenges is essential for responsible and effective AI implementation in supply chain management. As AI continues to evolve, its role in supply chain optimization will expand, offering new opportunities and innovations for businesses to explore.

4.3 AI in Financial Services: Risk Management and Fraud Detection

Artificial Intelligence (AI) has profoundly impacted the financial services industry, particularly in the realms of risk management and fraud detection. By leveraging advanced algorithms, machine learning, and data analytics, financial institutions can enhance their ability to manage risks, prevent fraud, and safeguard their operations. This section delves into how AI is transforming these critical areas and the benefits it provides to financial services organizations.

AI in Risk Management

Risk management is a core function in the financial services industry, encompassing various types of risk, including credit risk, market risk, and operational risk. AI enhances risk management by providing advanced tools for analysis, prediction, and mitigation.

- **Credit Risk Assessment**: AI algorithms analyze a wide range of data sources, including financial history, transaction patterns, and alternative data, to assess the creditworthiness of borrowers. Machine learning models can identify subtle patterns and correlations that traditional credit scoring models might miss. For instance, AI can analyze social media activity or mobile phone usage to provide additional insights into a borrower's credit risk. Companies like Zest AI and Upstart use AI for more accurate and comprehensive credit risk assessment.

- **Market Risk Prediction**: AI tools predict market risks by analyzing historical data, market trends, and economic indicators. Machine learning models can forecast potential market fluctuations and identify emerging risks based on real-time data. This predictive capability enables financial institutions to make informed investment decisions and manage their portfolios more effectively. Firms like BlackRock and Bloomberg use AI for market risk prediction and portfolio management.

- **Operational Risk Management**: AI enhances operational risk management by analyzing internal data to identify potential operational failures and inefficiencies. AI systems can monitor transactions, detect anomalies, and provide alerts for potential operational risks. For example, AI can identify discrepancies in transaction records that may indicate operational issues or inefficiencies. Companies like IBM and SAS provide AI-driven solutions for operational risk management.

AI in Fraud Detection

Fraud detection is a critical area in financial services, as fraudulent activities can lead to significant financial losses and reputational damage. AI plays a pivotal role in detecting and preventing fraud by analyzing large volumes of data and identifying suspicious patterns.

- **Anomaly Detection**: AI algorithms analyze transaction data to detect anomalies that may indicate fraudulent activity. Machine learning models learn from historical fraud data to identify unusual patterns, such as unexpected transactions or deviations from normal behavior. For example, credit card companies use AI to detect unusual spending patterns that may signal fraudulent use. Companies like Mastercard and Visa utilize AI for real-time fraud detection and prevention.
- **Behavioral Analytics**: AI-driven behavioral analytics analyze customer behavior to detect potential fraud. By monitoring patterns in customer

interactions, transaction history, and account activities, AI can identify deviations that may suggest fraudulent behavior. For instance, AI can detect if an account is being accessed from an unusual location or device, indicating potential fraud. Solutions from firms like Riskified and Forter leverage AI for behavioral analytics and fraud prevention.

- **Identity Verification**: AI enhances identity verification processes by using biometric data, such as facial recognition and fingerprint scanning, to authenticate users. AI systems can analyze biometric data in real time to verify identities and prevent unauthorized access. For example, banks use AI-driven biometric authentication for secure access to accounts and transactions. Companies like Face++ and NexID provide AI-powered identity verification solutions.

AI in Financial Crime Prevention

In addition to traditional fraud detection, AI is increasingly used to combat various forms of financial crime, including money laundering and terrorist financing.

- **Anti-Money Laundering (AML)**: AI systems analyze transaction data and customer profiles to detect suspicious activities that may indicate money laundering. Machine learning models can identify complex money laundering schemes by analyzing transaction patterns and networks. For instance, AI can detect unusual patterns in transactions that may suggest money laundering activities. Solutions like Actimize and ComplyAdvantage offer AI-driven AML tools to prevent financial crime.

- **Terrorist Financing Detection**: AI tools monitor financial transactions and customer activities to detect potential terrorist financing activities. By analyzing transaction data, customer profiles, and external information sources, AI can identify patterns associated with terrorist financing. For example, AI can flag transactions that match known terrorist financing patterns or involve high-risk countries. Companies like Refinitiv and Palantir provide AI-powered solutions for detecting terrorist financing.

Benefits of AI in Risk Management and Fraud Detection

- **Enhanced Accuracy**: AI improves the accuracy of risk assessments and fraud detection by analyzing large volumes of data and identifying subtle patterns. Machine learning models continuously learn and adapt, leading to more precise predictions and detections.

- **Real-Time Monitoring**: AI enables real-time monitoring of transactions and activities, allowing financial institutions to detect and respond to potential issues promptly. This real-time capability enhances the effectiveness of fraud prevention and risk management efforts.

- **Cost Efficiency**: AI reduces the need for manual intervention by automating risk assessment and fraud detection processes. This automation lowers operational costs and improves efficiency in managing risks and preventing fraud.

- **Scalability**: AI solutions can scale to handle large volumes of data and transactions, making them suitable for financial institutions of all sizes. As transaction volumes and data complexity increase, AI systems can adapt and continue to provide effective risk management and fraud detection.

Ethical Considerations and Challenges

As AI becomes integral to risk management and fraud detection, financial institutions must address ethical considerations and challenges related to data privacy, transparency, and bias.

- **Data Privacy**: AI-driven risk management and fraud detection rely on extensive data collection and analysis. Financial institutions must ensure compliance with data privacy regulations, such as GDPR and CCPA, and implement robust data protection measures to safeguard customer information.
- **Transparency**: Transparency in AI decision-making is essential for building trust with stakeholders. Financial institutions should provide clear explanations of how AI models make decisions and ensure that the decision-making process is understandable and accountable.
- **Bias and Fairness**: AI models can inadvertently introduce biases based on the data they are trained on. Financial institutions must regularly evaluate and address biases in AI systems to ensure fair and equitable treatment of all customers. Ethical AI practices and ongoing audits can help mitigate potential biases.

AI has revolutionized risk management and fraud detection in financial services by providing advanced tools for analysis, prediction, and prevention. Through applications such as credit risk assessment, market risk prediction, anomaly detection, and anti-money laundering, AI enhances the ability of financial institutions to manage risks, prevent fraud, and ensure secure operations. Addressing ethical considerations and challenges is crucial for responsible and effective AI implementation. As AI technology continues to evolve, its role in financial services will expand, offering new opportunities for innovation and improvement in risk management and fraud detection.

4.4 Human Resources and Talent Management Using AI

Artificial Intelligence (AI) is transforming Human Resources (HR) and talent management by streamlining processes, enhancing decision-making, and improving employee experiences. AI technologies offer powerful tools for various HR functions, from recruitment and onboarding to performance management and employee retention. This section explores how AI is revolutionizing HR practices and the benefits it brings to organizations and their workforce.

195

Recruitment and talent acquisition are critical functions of HR, and AI significantly enhances these processes by improving efficiency and accuracy.

- **Resume Screening and Shortlisting**: AI-powered resume screening tools use natural language processing (NLP) and machine learning algorithms to analyze and rank resumes based on job requirements and qualifications. These tools can quickly identify the most suitable candidates from large volumes of applications, reducing the time and effort required for manual screening. For example, platforms like HireVue and Pymetrics use AI to streamline resume screening and candidate shortlisting.

- **Candidate Sourcing**: AI tools assist in sourcing candidates by analyzing online profiles, social media activity, and professional networks to identify potential talent. AI algorithms can match candidate profiles with job openings and recommend suitable candidates to recruiters. Solutions like LinkedIn Recruiter and Entelo leverage AI for candidate sourcing and engagement.

- **Interview Scheduling and Coordination**: AI-powered chatbots and scheduling tools automate the process of scheduling interviews and coordinating with candidates. These tools can handle multiple scheduling requests, send reminders, and manage interview logistics, saving time for HR professionals. Companies like X0PA AI and Talview offer AI-driven interview scheduling solutions.

- **Predictive Analytics for Hiring**: AI systems use predictive analytics to assess the potential success of candidates based on historical data and performance metrics. Machine learning models can predict which candidates are likely to excel in specific roles, helping organizations make informed hiring decisions. For instance, predictive analytics tools can analyze past hiring data to identify traits associated with high-performing employees.

AI in Onboarding and Training

Onboarding and training are essential for integrating new employees and developing their skills. AI enhances these processes by providing personalized and efficient solutions.

- **Personalized Onboarding Experiences**: AI-driven onboarding platforms create customized onboarding experiences for new hires by tailoring content and resources based on individual roles and preferences. These platforms can provide interactive training modules, introduce new employees to company culture, and facilitate smooth transitions. Solutions like Sapling and Talmundo offer AI-powered onboarding experiences.

- **AI-Powered Learning and Development**: AI tools deliver personalized training programs by analyzing employees' skills, learning styles, and career goals. Machine learning algorithms can recommend relevant courses, track progress, and provide feedback to enhance learning outcomes. For example, platforms like Coursera and Udacity use AI to offer tailored learning paths and skill development opportunities.

- **Virtual Coaching and Support**: AI-powered virtual coaches provide real-time support and guidance to employees, addressing questions and offering career advice. These virtual assistants can assist with skill development, performance improvement, and career planning. Companies like

CoachAccountable and BetterUp use AI for virtual coaching and employee support.

AI in Performance Management

Performance management is crucial for evaluating employee performance and driving development. AI enhances performance management by providing data-driven insights and objective evaluations.

- **Performance Analytics**: AI systems analyze performance data, including key performance indicators (KPIs), feedback, and goal attainment, to assess employee performance. These systems can identify patterns, trends, and areas for improvement, helping managers make data-driven decisions. Tools like Lattice and 15Five leverage AI for performance analytics and management.

- **Continuous Feedback and Evaluation**: AI-driven platforms facilitate continuous feedback and performance evaluations by gathering real-time input from peers, managers, and employees. These platforms provide actionable insights and recommendations for performance improvement and career development. Solutions like Culture

Amp and TinyPulse use AI for continuous feedback and performance evaluation.

- **Goal Setting and Tracking**: AI tools help set and track employee goals by analyzing performance data and aligning goals with organizational objectives. Machine learning algorithms can provide insights into goal achievement and suggest adjustments to ensure alignment with company priorities. Platforms like OKR Tracker and Weekdone use AI for goal setting and tracking.

AI in Employee Engagement and Retention

Employee engagement and retention are vital for maintaining a motivated and productive workforce. AI supports these areas by enhancing employee experiences and addressing potential issues.

- **Employee Sentiment Analysis**: AI-powered sentiment analysis tools analyze employee feedback, surveys, and communication to gauge overall sentiment and identify areas of concern. These tools can detect issues such as low morale or dissatisfaction and provide recommendations for improvement. Solutions like Glint and Qualtrics use

AI for employee sentiment analysis and engagement.

- **Predictive Retention Analytics**: AI models predict employee turnover and identify factors that contribute to retention or attrition. By analyzing historical data and employee behavior, AI can help organizations implement strategies to retain top talent and reduce turnover. Companies like Visier and Workday offer AI-driven retention analytics solutions.

- **Personalized Employee Experiences**: AI enhances employee experiences by providing personalized recommendations for career development, work-life balance, and well-being. AI tools can analyze employee preferences and needs to offer tailored solutions and support. Platforms like Achievers and Officevibe use AI for personalized employee engagement and well-being.

Ethical Considerations and Challenges

As AI becomes integral to HR and talent management, organizations must address ethical considerations and challenges related to data privacy, transparency, and bias.

- **Data Privacy**: AI-driven HR solutions rely on extensive employee data, including personal and performance information. Organizations must ensure compliance with data privacy regulations, such as GDPR and CCPA, and implement robust data protection measures to safeguard employee information.

- **Transparency**: Transparency in AI decision-making is crucial for building trust with employees. Organizations should provide clear explanations of how AI models make decisions and ensure that employees understand how their data is used.

- **Bias and Fairness**: AI models can inadvertently introduce biases based on the data they are trained on. Organizations must regularly evaluate and address biases in AI systems to ensure fair and equitable treatment of all employees. Ethical AI practices and ongoing audits can help mitigate potential biases.

AI is transforming HR and talent management by enhancing recruitment, onboarding, performance management, and employee engagement. Through applications such as resume screening, personalized onboarding, performance analytics, and predictive retention analytics, AI provides valuable tools for improving HR processes and employee experiences. Addressing ethical considerations and challenges is essential for responsible and effective AI implementation. As AI technology continues to evolve, its role in HR and talent management will expand, offering new opportunities for innovation and improvement in workforce management.

4.5 AI-Driven Innovation in Product Development

Artificial Intelligence (AI) is reshaping product development by driving innovation, accelerating design processes, and enhancing product quality. By leveraging advanced algorithms, machine learning, and data analytics, organizations can streamline their product development lifecycle, from ideation to market launch. This section explores how AI is revolutionizing product development and the benefits it offers to businesses and consumers.

AI in Product Ideation and Concept Generation

Product ideation and concept generation are critical stages in the product development lifecycle. AI enhances these processes by providing insights and facilitating creativity.

- **Idea Generation and Trend Analysis**: AI tools analyze market trends, consumer preferences, and competitive landscapes to generate innovative product ideas. By processing vast amounts of data from social media, online reviews, and industry reports, AI can identify emerging trends and suggest potential product concepts. Platforms like Trendalytics and Crayon leverage AI for trend analysis and idea generation.

- **Customer Insights and Feedback**: AI systems analyze customer feedback, reviews, and surveys to uncover insights into consumer needs and preferences. Machine learning algorithms can identify patterns in customer sentiment and behavior, helping businesses develop products that align with market demands. For example, AI can analyze customer feedback to identify pain points and opportunities for new product features.

- **Generative Design**: AI-driven generative design tools create multiple design options based on specified parameters and constraints. These tools use algorithms to explore various design alternatives and optimize for performance, cost, and manufacturability. Companies like Autodesk and

Dassault Systèmes offer AI-powered generative design solutions that accelerate concept development and innovation.

AI in Product Design and Development

AI accelerates product design and development by automating processes, improving accuracy, and enhancing collaboration.

- **Automated Design and Prototyping**: AI tools automate the design and prototyping processes by generating digital models and simulations. Machine learning algorithms can optimize designs for performance, safety, and efficiency, reducing the need for manual adjustments. For instance, AI-driven software can create virtual prototypes and simulate real-world conditions to test product performance.
- **Design Optimization and Validation**: AI algorithms analyze design parameters and performance metrics to optimize product designs. These algorithms can identify potential issues and suggest improvements, ensuring that products meet quality standards and regulatory requirements.

Solutions like Ansys and Altair use AI for design optimization and validation in various industries.

- **Collaborative Design Platforms**: AI-powered collaborative design platforms facilitate communication and coordination among design teams. These platforms use AI to manage design changes, track progress, and integrate feedback from multiple stakeholders. Tools like SolidWorks and Onshape offer AI-driven collaboration features for product design and development.

AI in Product Testing and Quality Assurance

Product testing and quality assurance are essential for ensuring that products meet performance and safety standards. AI enhances these processes by improving accuracy and efficiency.

- **Predictive Testing and Simulation**: AI-driven predictive testing tools simulate product performance under various conditions and predict potential failures. Machine learning models analyze historical testing data to identify patterns and forecast issues, allowing businesses to address problems before physical testing. Platforms like

Siemens and Comsol use AI for predictive testing and simulation.

- **Automated Quality Control**: AI-powered quality control systems use computer vision and machine learning to inspect products for defects and inconsistencies. These systems can analyze images and detect anomalies with high precision, reducing the need for manual inspections. Companies like Cognex and Keyence offer AI-driven quality control solutions for manufacturing.

- **Real-Time Monitoring and Feedback**: AI tools monitor product performance in real time and provide feedback on quality metrics. By analyzing data from sensors and IoT devices, AI can detect deviations from expected performance and trigger corrective actions. Solutions like Honeywell and GE Digital leverage AI for real-time monitoring and quality assurance.

AI in Product Personalization and Customization

AI enables personalized and customized product offerings by analyzing individual preferences and tailoring products to meet specific needs.

- **Personalized Recommendations**: AI-driven recommendation systems analyze customer behavior and preferences to suggest personalized product options. These systems can enhance the customer experience by providing relevant recommendations based on past purchases, browsing history, and demographic data. Companies like Amazon and Netflix use AI for personalized recommendations in their product offerings.

- **Custom Product Configurations**: AI tools enable customers to configure and customize products according to their specifications. By using AI algorithms to manage customization options and ensure compatibility, businesses can offer personalized products that meet individual needs. Platforms like MyCustomizer and Threekit provide AI-driven product customization solutions.

- **Adaptive Product Features**: AI technologies enable products to adapt to user preferences and behavior over time. Machine learning algorithms can analyze user interactions and adjust product features to enhance functionality and usability. For example, smart home devices use AI to learn user preferences and optimize settings for comfort and convenience.

AI in Product Lifecycle Management

AI supports product lifecycle management by providing insights and optimizing processes throughout a product's lifecycle.

- **Lifecycle Analytics and Forecasting**: AI-driven analytics tools provide insights into product performance and lifecycle trends. Machine learning models analyze data from various sources to forecast product demand, sales trends, and end-of-life stages. Solutions like PTC and SAP offer AI-powered lifecycle analytics and forecasting tools.

- **Maintenance and Support**: AI enhances product maintenance and support by predicting maintenance needs and providing proactive solutions. Predictive maintenance algorithms analyze usage data and performance metrics to identify potential issues and schedule maintenance activities. Companies like IBM and ServiceMax use AI for predictive maintenance and support.

- **End-of-Life Management**: AI tools assist in managing a product's end-of-life stage by analyzing market trends and customer feedback to inform decisions about product discontinuation and replacement. These tools can provide recommendations for phasing out products and transitioning to new offerings. Solutions like Agile and Arena offer AI-driven end-of-life management tools.

Ethical Considerations and Challenges

As AI becomes integral to product development, organizations must address ethical considerations and challenges related to data privacy, transparency, and bias.

- **Data Privacy**: AI-driven product development relies on extensive data collection and analysis. Organizations must ensure compliance with data privacy regulations, such as GDPR and CCPA, and implement robust data protection measures to safeguard customer information.
- **Transparency**: Transparency in AI decision-making is crucial for building trust with stakeholders. Organizations should provide clear

explanations of how AI models make decisions and ensure that the decision-making process is understandable and accountable.

- **Bias and Fairness**: AI models can inadvertently introduce biases based on the data they are trained on. Organizations must regularly evaluate and address biases in AI systems to ensure fair and equitable treatment of all customers and users. Ethical AI practices and ongoing audits can help mitigate potential biases.

AI-driven innovation is transforming product development by enhancing ideation, design, testing, personalization, and lifecycle management. Through applications such as generative design, predictive testing, and personalized recommendations, AI provides valuable tools for accelerating product development and improving product quality. Addressing ethical considerations and challenges is essential for responsible and effective AI implementation. As AI technology continues to evolve, its role in product development will expand, offering new opportunities for innovation and improvement in the development and delivery of products.

Chapter 5: The Future of AI in Decision Making: Opportunities and Challenges

- 5.1 Emerging Trends in AI Technologies
- 5.2 Ethical Considerations in AI-Powered Decision Making
- 5.3 The Impact of AI on Jobs and Workforce Transformation

Chapter 5: The Future of AI in Decision Making: Opportunities and Challenges

Chapter 5 explores the evolving landscape of AI-driven decision making, focusing on the opportunities and challenges that lie ahead. As AI continues to reshape industries, this chapter examines how organizations can harness emerging technologies to further enhance their decision-making processes while navigating the complexities that come with these advancements. The chapter begins by discussing **emerging trends in AI technologies**, such as advancements in deep learning, reinforcement learning, and AI-driven automation. These innovations offer businesses new opportunities to leverage AI for more sophisticated decision-making capabilities, such as optimizing complex systems, predicting market shifts, and responding in real-time to dynamic business environments. The chapter highlights how staying ahead of these technological trends will be key to maintaining a competitive edge. In parallel, the chapter explores the **ethical considerations** surrounding AI-powered decision making. As AI becomes more embedded in critical decision processes, questions about transparency, fairness, and accountability arise. Issues such as algorithmic bias, data privacy, and the ethical use of AI in decision-making frameworks are addressed, emphasizing the importance of responsible AI development and deployment.

The impact of AI on the workforce is another crucial aspect covered in this chapter. **AI's role in workforce transformation** is explored, examining how automation will change job roles, create new opportunities, and require reskilling and upskilling of employees. The chapter stresses the importance of balancing AI adoption with human-centered approaches, ensuring that employees can work alongside AI technologies rather than being replaced by them. Finally, the chapter covers **regulatory frameworks and policies** for AI in business, recognizing the growing need for global standards and regulations to guide the ethical and fair use of AI. It also offers insights on how businesses can **prepare for an AI-driven future**, building adaptable, resilient strategies that take advantage of AI's potential while managing the associated risks. Chapter 5 provides a forward-looking perspective on AI in decision making, offering a balanced view of the opportunities it presents and the challenges businesses must overcome to thrive in an increasingly AI-driven world.

Introduction

Artificial Intelligence (AI) is poised to shape the future of decision-making across various domains, offering unprecedented opportunities for efficiency, accuracy, and innovation. As AI technologies continue to advance, they present both exciting possibilities and significant challenges. This chapter explores the potential of AI to transform decision-making processes, the opportunities it creates, and the challenges that need to be addressed to fully realize its benefits.

The Evolution of AI in Decision Making

AI has already made substantial inroads into decision-making processes, from business and healthcare to finance and public policy. The evolution of AI in decision-making has been marked by several key developments:

- **Advancements in Machine Learning**: The evolution of machine learning algorithms has enabled AI systems to learn from data and make predictions with increasing accuracy. Techniques such as deep learning, reinforcement learning, and ensemble methods have advanced decision-making capabilities by processing complex datasets and uncovering hidden patterns.
- **Integration of Big Data**: The proliferation of big data has provided AI systems with vast amounts of information to analyze. AI's ability to process and analyze large-scale data sets has enhanced decision-making by providing more comprehensive insights and facilitating real-time analysis.

- **Enhanced Computational Power**: The growth in computational power, driven by advances in hardware and cloud computing, has enabled more sophisticated AI models to operate efficiently. Increased processing capabilities have allowed for more complex algorithms and larger datasets, improving the accuracy and speed of decision-making.

Opportunities for AI-Driven Decision Making

AI presents numerous opportunities for enhancing decision-making across various domains. These opportunities include:

- **Improved Predictive Analytics**: AI enhances predictive analytics by analyzing historical data and identifying trends that can forecast future outcomes. This capability is particularly valuable in fields such as finance, healthcare, and marketing, where accurate predictions can drive strategic decisions. For example, AI can predict stock market trends, patient outcomes, and consumer behavior, enabling more informed decision-making.

- **Enhanced Decision Support Systems**: AI-driven decision support systems provide valuable insights and recommendations to aid human decision-makers. These systems can analyze complex scenarios, evaluate alternatives, and offer evidence-based suggestions, improving the quality of decisions. In healthcare, for instance, AI can assist doctors in diagnosing diseases and recommending treatments based on patient data.

- **Automation of Routine Decisions**: AI can automate routine and repetitive decision-making processes, freeing up human resources for more strategic tasks. Automation of decisions such as inventory management, fraud detection, and customer service responses can lead to increased efficiency and cost savings.

- **Personalized Experiences**: AI enables the creation of personalized experiences by analyzing individual preferences and behavior. In sectors such as e-commerce and entertainment, AI can tailor recommendations and content to individual users, enhancing customer satisfaction and engagement.

- **Real-Time Decision Making**: AI systems can analyze data in real-time and provide immediate insights, enabling timely decision-making in dynamic environments. For example, AI can monitor and respond to real-time traffic conditions, market fluctuations, and cybersecurity threats, allowing for rapid adjustments and interventions.

Challenges in AI-Driven Decision Making

Despite the numerous opportunities, AI-driven decision making also presents several challenges that need to be addressed:

- **Data Privacy and Security**: The reliance on large volumes of data raises concerns about data privacy and security. Ensuring that data is collected, stored, and processed in compliance with privacy regulations is crucial to protecting sensitive information and maintaining public trust.
- **Bias and Fairness**: AI systems can inadvertently introduce biases based on the data they are trained on. Addressing bias and ensuring fairness in AI decision-making is essential to prevent discriminatory outcomes and ensure equitable treatment for all individuals. Regular audits and

diverse datasets can help mitigate biases in AI
models.

- **Transparency and Explainability**: The
complexity of AI algorithms can make it
challenging to understand how decisions are made.
Enhancing transparency and explainability in AI
systems is important for building trust and ensuring
that stakeholders can comprehend and challenge AI-
driven decisions. Efforts to develop interpretable AI
models and provide clear explanations of decision
processes are ongoing.

- **Ethical and Legal Implications**: The use of AI in
decision-making raises ethical and legal questions,
such as accountability for AI-driven decisions and
the potential for misuse. Developing ethical
guidelines and legal frameworks to govern the use
of AI is crucial for addressing these concerns and
ensuring responsible AI practices.

- **Integration with Human Decision-Making**: While
AI can provide valuable insights, it is essential to
integrate AI with human decision-making processes
effectively. Striking the right balance between AI-
driven recommendations and human judgment is
important for making well-rounded decisions and

addressing complex scenarios that may require human expertise.

Future Directions and Emerging Trends

The future of AI in decision-making will likely be shaped by several emerging trends and developments:

- **Advances in Explainable AI (XAI)**: Efforts to develop explainable AI models will continue to enhance transparency and understanding of AI decision-making processes. Explainable AI aims to make AI systems more interpretable and accessible to users, promoting trust and accountability.

- **Increased Collaboration between AI and Humans**: The future will see greater collaboration between AI systems and human decision-makers. AI will act as a powerful tool to support and augment human decision-making, rather than replace it. Collaborative approaches will leverage the strengths of both AI and human expertise.

- **Expansion of AI Applications**: AI will expand its applications across various domains, including healthcare, finance, manufacturing, and public policy. As AI technologies advance, new opportunities will arise for applying AI to address complex challenges and drive innovation.

- **Focus on Ethical AI**: There will be a growing emphasis on developing ethical AI practices and addressing the social and ethical implications of AI. Organizations and policymakers will work towards establishing frameworks and standards to ensure responsible and ethical use of AI in decision-making.

- **Integration of AI with Emerging Technologies**: AI will increasingly be integrated with other emerging technologies, such as blockchain, IoT, and augmented reality. This integration will create new possibilities for decision-making and drive advancements in various fields.

The future of AI in decision-making holds tremendous potential for enhancing efficiency, accuracy, and innovation. While AI presents numerous opportunities, it also comes with challenges that must be addressed to fully realize its benefits. By focusing on ethical considerations, transparency, and collaboration, organizations can harness the power of AI to drive informed decision-making and achieve positive outcomes. As AI technology continues to evolve, its role in decision-making will become increasingly integral, shaping the future of various industries and sectors.

5.1 Emerging Trends in AI Technologies

As Artificial Intelligence (AI) continues to evolve, several emerging trends are shaping the future of AI technologies. These trends are driving innovation, expanding the scope of AI applications, and transforming various industries. This section explores some of the most significant emerging trends in AI technologies and their potential impact.

1. Generative AI

Generative AI refers to the capability of AI systems to create new content, such as images, text, and music, based on existing data. This trend is revolutionizing creative industries and content generation by:

- **Advancing Creativity**: Generative AI models, such as Generative Adversarial Networks (GANs) and Variational Autoencoders (VAEs), can produce high-quality content that mimics human creativity. Applications include generating realistic images, writing coherent and contextually relevant text, and composing original music. For instance, OpenAI's

GPT-4 and DALL-E 2 have demonstrated impressive capabilities in generating human-like text and images.

- **Accelerating Design Processes**: In design and engineering, generative AI can create multiple design options based on specified parameters. This technology is used in product design, architecture, and urban planning to explore innovative solutions and optimize designs. Autodesk's generative design tools are examples of how AI can accelerate the design process.

- **Enhancing Personalization**: Generative AI enables highly personalized content and experiences by tailoring outputs to individual preferences and needs. This trend is evident in personalized marketing, content recommendations, and interactive entertainment.

2. Explainable AI (XAI)

Explainable AI (XAI) focuses on making AI systems more transparent and interpretable, allowing users to understand how decisions are made. This trend addresses the need for accountability and trust in AI:

- **Improving Trust and Adoption**: XAI aims to bridge the gap between complex AI models and user understanding. By providing clear explanations of AI decisions and processes, XAI enhances user trust and facilitates wider adoption of AI technologies. Research in XAI includes methods for visualizing model outputs and elucidating decision-making processes.

- **Regulatory Compliance**: As AI systems are increasingly subject to regulatory scrutiny, XAI helps organizations comply with data protection and transparency requirements. For example, the General Data Protection Regulation (GDPR) mandates the right to explanation for automated decisions, making XAI a critical area of focus.

- **Facilitating Debugging and Improvement**: XAI provides insights into how AI models operate, which can aid in debugging and refining algorithms. Understanding the factors influencing model decisions helps researchers and developers improve accuracy and performance.

3. AI in Edge Computing

Edge computing involves processing data closer to the source, rather than relying solely on centralized cloud servers. AI is increasingly being integrated into edge computing environments:

- **Reducing Latency**: By deploying AI models on edge devices, such as smartphones, IoT sensors, and industrial equipment, organizations can achieve lower latency and faster response times. Edge AI enables real-time decision-making in applications like autonomous vehicles, smart cities, and industrial automation.

- **Enhancing Privacy and Security**: Edge computing can improve data privacy and security by minimizing the need to transmit sensitive information to central servers. AI models running on edge devices can process data locally, reducing the risk of data breaches and unauthorized access.

- **Supporting Offline Operations**: AI-powered edge devices can operate independently of network connectivity, making them suitable for remote or offline environments. This capability is valuable in applications such as remote monitoring, field inspections, and disaster response.

4. AI-Driven Automation and Robotics

AI-driven automation and robotics are transforming industries by enhancing efficiency, precision, and productivity:

- **Advancing Industrial Automation**: AI-powered robots and automation systems are revolutionizing manufacturing and production processes. These systems can perform tasks with high accuracy, adapt to changing conditions, and optimize workflows. Companies like Boston Dynamics and ABB are at the forefront of AI-driven robotics.

- **Enabling Collaborative Robots**: Collaborative robots (cobots) work alongside human operators, enhancing productivity and safety in various settings. AI enables cobots to understand and respond to human actions, facilitating seamless collaboration and task automation.

- **Transforming Service Industries**: AI-driven automation is also impacting service industries, including healthcare, retail, and customer service. Robotic process automation (RPA) and AI chatbots are streamlining repetitive tasks, improving customer interactions, and supporting healthcare procedures.

5. AI and Quantum Computing

Quantum computing represents a new paradigm of computation with the potential to exponentially increase processing power. The intersection of AI and quantum computing holds significant promise:

- **Enhancing Computational Power**: Quantum computers can solve complex problems and process vast amounts of data at unprecedented speeds. This increased computational power can accelerate AI training, optimize algorithms, and enable new applications in areas such as drug discovery, cryptography, and materials science.

- **Exploring New AI Algorithms**: Quantum computing opens the door to novel AI algorithms and models that leverage quantum principles. Researchers are exploring quantum machine learning techniques that combine quantum computing with traditional AI approaches to address challenges beyond the capabilities of classical computers.

- **Overcoming Computational Limits**: AI applications that require extensive computational resources, such as deep learning and large-scale simulations, can benefit from quantum computing advancements. Quantum algorithms may overcome limitations associated with classical computing and unlock new possibilities in AI research and development.

6. Ethical AI and Responsible AI

Ethical AI and responsible AI practices are gaining prominence as organizations address the societal impact of AI technologies:

- **Promoting Fairness and Inclusivity**: Ethical AI focuses on ensuring that AI systems are fair, unbiased, and inclusive. Efforts include developing guidelines and frameworks for responsible AI use, addressing algorithmic bias, and promoting diversity in AI development teams.

- **Ensuring Accountability**: Responsible AI practices emphasize accountability for AI-driven decisions and actions. Organizations are establishing mechanisms for auditing, monitoring, and addressing the ethical implications of AI systems to ensure they align with societal values and legal standards.

- **Fostering Collaboration and Dialogue**: Engaging stakeholders, including policymakers, researchers, and the public, is essential for addressing ethical challenges and shaping the future of AI. Collaborative efforts aim to create standards and best practices that guide the development and deployment of AI technologies.

Emerging trends in AI technologies are driving significant advancements and transforming various aspects of our lives. From generative AI and explainable AI to edge computing and quantum computing, these trends offer exciting opportunities for innovation and improvement. At the same time, addressing ethical considerations and ensuring responsible AI practices are crucial for harnessing the benefits of AI while mitigating potential risks. As AI technologies continue to evolve, staying informed about these trends and their implications will be essential for navigating the future of AI-driven decision-making and technology.

5.2 Ethical Considerations in AI-Powered Decision Making

The integration of Artificial Intelligence (AI) into decision-making processes raises significant ethical considerations that must be carefully addressed to ensure responsible and fair use of technology. As AI systems become increasingly involved in critical decisions across various domains—such as healthcare, finance, and law enforcement—it is imperative to consider the ethical implications of these technologies. This section explores key ethical considerations in AI-powered decision-making and discusses strategies for addressing these concerns.

1. Bias and Fairness

AI systems can inadvertently perpetuate or even exacerbate biases present in the data they are trained on. Addressing bias and ensuring fairness is a fundamental ethical concern in AI decision-making:

- **Sources of Bias**: Bias in AI systems can stem from various sources, including biased training data, flawed algorithms, and subjective design choices. For example, if an AI model is trained on historical data reflecting societal biases, it may produce discriminatory outcomes, such as unfairly targeting certain demographic groups in credit scoring or hiring practices.

- **Mitigation Strategies**: To address bias, organizations must implement strategies such as diversifying training datasets, applying fairness-aware algorithms, and conducting regular audits of AI systems. Techniques like bias correction, adversarial debiasing, and differential privacy can help reduce the impact of biases and promote fairness.

- **Transparency and Accountability**: Transparency in AI decision-making processes is essential for identifying and addressing bias. Providing clear explanations of how decisions are made and involving diverse stakeholders in the development and evaluation of AI systems can help ensure accountability and fairness.

2. Privacy and Data Protection

The use of AI often involves processing large volumes of personal and sensitive data, raising concerns about privacy and data protection:

- **Data Collection and Usage**: AI systems require access to extensive data to function effectively. Organizations must ensure that data collection practices comply with privacy regulations, such as the General Data Protection Regulation (GDPR) and the California Consumer Privacy Act (CCPA). This includes obtaining informed consent, safeguarding data security, and limiting data usage to the intended purposes.

- **Data Anonymization**: Anonymizing data can help protect individuals' privacy by removing or obscuring personally identifiable information. Techniques such as data masking, aggregation, and pseudonymization can reduce the risk of privacy breaches while allowing AI systems to perform valuable analyses.

- **Data Ownership and Control**: Individuals should have control over their personal data and be informed about how it is used. Providing options for data access, correction, and deletion, as well as implementing robust data governance practices, can help address concerns related to data ownership and control.

3. Transparency and Explainability

AI decision-making processes are often complex and opaque, making it challenging for users to understand how decisions are made:

- **Explainable AI (XAI)**: Explainable AI aims to make AI systems more transparent by providing clear and interpretable explanations of their decisions. Techniques such as feature importance analysis, visualizations, and model-agnostic methods can help users comprehend AI outputs and build trust in the technology.

- **Impact on Decision-Making**: Transparency and explainability are crucial for ensuring that AI systems are used responsibly and that their decisions can be scrutinized. This is especially important in high-stakes applications, such as legal and medical contexts, where understanding the rationale behind AI decisions is essential for ensuring fairness and accountability.

- **Ethical Considerations**: Striving for explainability must balance the need for transparency with the potential risks of exposing sensitive information or proprietary algorithms. Organizations should consider the ethical implications of providing explanations and ensure that they do not compromise security or intellectual property.

4. Accountability and Responsibility

Assigning accountability for AI-driven decisions and actions is a key ethical consideration:

- **Responsibility for Outcomes**: Organizations must establish clear lines of responsibility for AI-driven decisions and ensure that human oversight is maintained. Decision-makers should be accountable for the outcomes of AI systems and address any negative consequences that arise.

- **Ethical Governance**: Implementing ethical governance frameworks can help organizations manage the ethical implications of AI. This includes establishing ethical guidelines, creating oversight committees, and developing protocols for handling ethical dilemmas and unintended consequences.

- **Regulatory Compliance**: Adhering to regulations and standards related to AI ethics is essential for ensuring responsible use of technology. Compliance with existing laws and participation in the development of new regulations can help organizations navigate ethical challenges and promote responsible AI practices.

5. Autonomy and Human Oversight

Maintaining human oversight and ensuring that AI systems support rather than replace human decision-making is an important ethical consideration:

- **Balancing Automation and Human Judgment**: AI should augment human decision-making rather than fully automate it. Human oversight is crucial for addressing complex, nuanced situations that AI systems may not fully comprehend. Ensuring that AI systems provide decision support rather than replacing human judgment can help maintain ethical standards.

- **Preventing Overreliance**: Overreliance on AI can lead to complacency and the neglect of critical thinking and ethical considerations. Organizations should promote a balanced approach that combines the strengths of AI with human expertise and ethical judgment.

- **Ensuring Human Agency**: Individuals should retain agency and control over decisions that affect their lives. AI systems should be designed to empower users and provide them with meaningful choices, rather than dictating outcomes without human input.

6. *Social and Economic Impacts*

AI's influence on society and the economy introduces additional ethical considerations:

- **Economic Displacement**: The automation of tasks and processes can lead to job displacement and changes in the workforce. Organizations should consider the social and economic impacts of AI, including strategies for reskilling and supporting affected workers.
- **Social Inequality**: AI technologies have the potential to exacerbate existing social inequalities if access to benefits is unevenly distributed. Ensuring equitable access to AI resources and addressing disparities in technology adoption can help mitigate social inequality.
- **Long-Term Consequences**: The long-term consequences of AI technologies, such as their impact on society, culture, and human behavior,

should be considered. Organizations and policymakers should anticipate potential future challenges and work towards creating a positive and inclusive AI-driven future.

Ethical considerations in AI-powered decision-making are critical for ensuring that AI technologies are used responsibly and fairly. Addressing issues such as bias, privacy, transparency, accountability, and the broader social impacts of AI is essential for fostering trust and promoting ethical practices. By implementing strategies to manage these ethical challenges and engaging in ongoing dialogue, organizations can navigate the complexities of AI decision-making and contribute to the development of a responsible and equitable AI-driven future.

5.3 The Impact of AI on Jobs and Workforce Transformation

The rise of Artificial Intelligence (AI) is reshaping the job market and transforming workforce dynamics across various industries. As AI technologies become more advanced and integrated into business processes, they are driving significant changes in how work is performed, which jobs are created or displaced, and how skills are valued. This section explores the multifaceted impact of AI on jobs and workforce transformation, highlighting both the opportunities and challenges presented by this technological shift.

1. Job Creation and New Opportunities

Despite concerns about job displacement, AI also creates new job opportunities and roles:

- **Emerging Job Roles**: The development and deployment of AI technologies have led to the creation of new job roles that did not previously exist. Examples include AI specialists, data scientists, machine learning engineers, and AI ethicists. These roles are essential for designing, implementing, and managing AI systems, as well as addressing ethical and regulatory considerations.

- **Increased Demand for Technical Skills**: AI's integration into various industries has heightened the demand for technical skills related to AI, machine learning, data analysis, and software development. Workers with expertise in these areas are in high demand, leading to new career prospects and opportunities for professional growth.

- **Innovation and Entrepreneurship**: AI fosters innovation and entrepreneurship by enabling new business models, products, and services. Startups and established companies alike are leveraging AI to create novel solutions and disrupt traditional markets, generating new job opportunities in sectors such as healthcare, finance, and retail.

- **Enhanced Productivity and Efficiency**: AI can augment human capabilities and enhance productivity, leading to the creation of more complex and strategic roles. For instance, AI-powered tools can automate repetitive tasks, allowing employees to focus on higher-value activities such as strategic planning, problem-solving, and creativity.

2. Job Displacement and Workforce Disruption

The automation of tasks and processes through AI can lead to job displacement and workforce disruption:

- **Automation of Routine Tasks**: AI technologies, such as robotic process automation (RPA) and machine learning algorithms, can automate routine and repetitive tasks across various industries. This automation can result in job displacement for roles involving manual or repetitive work, such as administrative assistants, data entry clerks, and assembly line workers.

- **Impact on Low-Skill Jobs**: Jobs that require lower levels of skill and involve routine procedures are particularly vulnerable to automation. As AI systems become more capable, there is a risk of job losses in sectors such as manufacturing, retail, and customer service, where tasks are often standardized and repetitive.

- **Shift in Job Requirements**: The skills and qualifications required for many jobs are evolving as AI technologies become more prevalent. Workers may need to acquire new skills and adapt to changing job requirements to remain relevant in the job market. This shift can create challenges for individuals who lack access to reskilling opportunities or face barriers to acquiring new competencies.

- **Economic and Social Impact**: Job displacement due to AI can have broader economic and social implications, including increased unemployment, income inequality, and social unrest. Addressing these impacts requires comprehensive strategies to support affected workers and communities, including social safety nets and targeted interventions.

3. Skills and Education for the AI Era

Adapting to the changing job market requires a focus on skills development and education:

- **Reskilling and Upskilling**: To navigate the impact of AI on jobs, workers need opportunities for reskilling and upskilling. Training programs and educational initiatives should focus on equipping individuals with skills relevant to the AI-driven economy, such as digital literacy, data analysis, and critical thinking.
- **Lifelong Learning**: The rapid pace of technological change necessitates a commitment to lifelong learning. Workers should be encouraged to engage in continuous education and professional development to stay current with evolving industry trends and technological advancements.
- **Collaborative Partnerships**: Collaboration between educational institutions, businesses, and

government agencies is crucial for developing effective training programs and addressing skills gaps. Partnerships can help align educational curricula with industry needs and ensure that workers are prepared for emerging job roles.

- **Focus on Soft Skills**: In addition to technical skills, soft skills such as problem-solving, communication, and adaptability are increasingly valuable in the AI era. These skills complement technical expertise and enable individuals to thrive in roles that require human judgment and interaction.

4. Workplace Transformation and Organizational Change

AI is transforming the workplace and organizational structures:

- **Enhanced Decision-Making**: AI tools and analytics can support data-driven decision-making, enabling organizations to make more informed and strategic choices. AI-driven insights can improve operational efficiency, customer engagement, and competitive advantage.
- **Flexible Work Arrangements**: AI technologies, such as collaboration tools and virtual assistants,

facilitate remote and flexible work arrangements. Organizations are increasingly adopting hybrid work models and leveraging AI to support virtual collaboration and productivity.

- **Changes in Management Practices**: The integration of AI into business processes may lead to changes in management practices and organizational structures. Managers may need to adapt to new workflows, oversee AI-driven initiatives, and ensure effective integration of AI technologies with human resources.

- **Ethical and Cultural Considerations**: As AI transforms the workplace, organizations must address ethical and cultural considerations related to AI implementation. This includes fostering a culture of transparency, ensuring ethical use of AI, and addressing potential biases in AI systems.

5. Policy and Support Measures

Governments and organizations play a crucial role in addressing the impact of AI on jobs and workforce transformation:

- **Policy Development**: Governments should develop policies that support workforce transitions, promote reskilling and upskilling, and address the economic and social impacts of AI. Policy measures may include unemployment benefits, training programs, and incentives for companies that invest in workforce development.

- **Social Safety Nets**: Strengthening social safety nets and support systems is essential for mitigating the negative effects of job displacement. Measures such as income support, job placement services, and career counseling can help individuals navigate transitions and find new opportunities.

- **Public-Private Collaboration**: Collaboration between the public and private sectors can enhance efforts to address workforce challenges. Public-private partnerships can support initiatives such as job training programs, research on future skills, and the development of industry standards.

- **Fostering Innovation**: Supporting innovation and entrepreneurship can create new job opportunities and drive economic growth. Governments and organizations can provide funding, resources, and support for startups and initiatives that leverage AI to address societal challenges and create value.

The impact of AI on jobs and workforce transformation is profound and multifaceted. While AI presents opportunities for job creation and enhanced productivity, it also poses challenges related to job displacement, skills requirements, and economic disruption. Addressing these challenges requires a concerted effort to support reskilling and upskilling, adapt to changing job requirements, and implement policies that promote a fair and inclusive transition to the AI-driven economy. By proactively managing the impact of AI and fostering collaboration among stakeholders, society can navigate the complexities of workforce transformation and harness the benefits of AI for a more equitable and prosperous future.

5.4 Regulatory Frameworks and Policies for AI in Business

As Artificial Intelligence (AI) becomes increasingly integral to business operations and decision-making, the need for robust regulatory frameworks and policies to guide its ethical and responsible use has become more pressing. These frameworks and policies aim to address various aspects of AI deployment, including transparency, accountability, data protection, and fairness. This section explores key regulatory frameworks and policies for AI in business, highlighting their objectives, challenges, and implementation strategies.

1. Global Regulatory Landscape

The regulatory landscape for AI varies significantly across regions and countries, reflecting diverse approaches to managing the technology's impact:

- **European Union (EU)**: The EU has taken a leading role in developing comprehensive AI regulations. The European Commission's Artificial Intelligence Act (AI Act), proposed in April 2021, is a landmark regulation aimed at ensuring that AI systems used within the EU are safe, transparent, and respect fundamental rights. The AI Act classifies AI systems into risk categories—unacceptable risk, high risk, and low risk—and imposes varying levels of requirements based on these categories. High-risk AI applications, such as those in healthcare and critical infrastructure, face stringent compliance requirements, including risk assessments, transparency obligations, and human oversight.

- **United States (US)**: In the US, the regulatory approach to AI is more fragmented and sector-specific. While there is no overarching federal AI regulation, various agencies and initiatives address AI-related issues. The National Institute of Standards and Technology (NIST) has developed a Framework for AI Risk Management to guide organizations in managing AI risks. Additionally, state-level regulations, such as California's Consumer Privacy Act (CCPA) and New York's proposed AI regulation, address specific aspects of AI, including data privacy and algorithmic accountability.

- **China**: China has also been active in regulating AI, with a focus on fostering innovation while managing risks. The Chinese government's New Generation Artificial Intelligence Development Plan emphasizes AI development and application, while the Measures for the Management of Algorithm Recommendation Services aim to regulate algorithmic transparency and content recommendation systems. China's approach combines support for AI advancement with regulatory measures to address data security and social impact.

2. Key Regulatory Areas

Several key areas are commonly addressed by AI regulations and policies:

- **Transparency and Explainability**: Regulations often require that AI systems provide clear and understandable explanations for their decisions. This is essential for ensuring that users can comprehend how AI systems operate and make informed decisions based on AI outputs. Transparency requirements may include providing information on algorithmic processes, data sources, and decision-making criteria.

- **Data Protection and Privacy**: Data protection regulations, such as the GDPR and CCPA, impose requirements on how organizations collect, store, and use personal data. For AI systems, this includes ensuring data privacy, obtaining consent for data usage, and implementing measures to protect sensitive information. Regulations may also address issues related to data ownership and the right to data access and deletion.

- **Bias and Fairness**: AI regulations aim to prevent and mitigate biases in AI systems to ensure fair treatment of individuals and groups. This involves implementing measures to detect and address algorithmic bias, conducting impact assessments, and promoting fairness-aware practices in AI development and deployment.

- **Accountability and Liability**: Establishing accountability and liability frameworks is crucial for addressing issues related to AI system failures and unintended consequences. Regulations may define the responsibilities of AI developers, users, and other stakeholders, and establish mechanisms for addressing grievances and compensating affected parties.

- **Ethical Use and Human Oversight**: Regulations may mandate ethical guidelines for AI use, including ensuring that AI systems are designed and deployed in ways that align with societal values and respect human rights. Human oversight requirements may include ensuring that AI decisions are subject to human review and intervention, particularly in high-stakes applications.

3. *Challenges in Implementing AI Regulations*

Implementing AI regulations poses several challenges:

- **Rapid Technological Advancements**: The fast pace of AI development makes it challenging for regulators to keep up with technological changes. Regulations may struggle to address emerging AI applications and innovations, requiring ongoing updates and adaptations.

- **Global Harmonization**: The fragmented regulatory landscape across different regions can create challenges for multinational businesses. Navigating varying regulations and compliance requirements can be complex and costly. Efforts toward global harmonization and international cooperation are essential for addressing these challenges.

- **Balancing Innovation and Regulation**: Regulators face the challenge of balancing the need for oversight with the need to foster innovation. Overly stringent regulations may stifle technological advancement, while inadequate regulation may lead to ethical and societal concerns. Striking the right balance is crucial for promoting responsible AI development.

- **Technical Complexity**: AI systems are complex and often involve proprietary algorithms and data. Ensuring that regulations effectively address technical aspects of AI while respecting intellectual property and trade secrets can be difficult. Technical expertise and collaboration with industry experts are essential for developing effective regulations.

4. Best Practices for Compliance

Organizations can adopt best practices to ensure compliance with AI regulations and policies:

- **Conducting Risk Assessments**: Organizations should perform regular risk assessments to identify and address potential compliance issues related to AI systems. This includes evaluating the impact of AI applications on privacy, fairness, and transparency.
- **Implementing Transparency Measures**: Providing clear information about AI systems,

including their functionality, data usage, and decision-making processes, helps meet transparency requirements and build trust with users.

- **Ensuring Data Protection**: Organizations should implement robust data protection measures, including data encryption, access controls, and privacy policies. Compliance with data protection regulations should be integrated into AI system design and operations.

- **Promoting Ethical Practices**: Adopting ethical guidelines and best practices for AI development and deployment helps ensure that AI systems are used responsibly and in alignment with societal values. This includes addressing algorithmic bias and ensuring human oversight.

- **Engaging with Regulators and Stakeholders**: Engaging with regulators, industry groups, and other stakeholders can provide valuable insights into regulatory developments and help shape effective policies. Collaboration and feedback can contribute to the development of balanced and practical regulations.

Regulatory frameworks and policies for AI in business are essential for ensuring the responsible and ethical use of AI technologies. Addressing key areas such as transparency, data protection, bias, and accountability helps create a regulatory environment that promotes trust and fairness while supporting innovation. As AI continues to evolve, ongoing efforts to develop and refine regulations, address implementation challenges, and adopt best practices will be crucial for navigating the complexities of AI governance and fostering a positive impact on society and the economy.

5.5 Preparing Your Organization for an AI-Driven Future

As organizations increasingly embrace Artificial Intelligence (AI), preparing for an AI-driven future is crucial for maintaining competitive advantage and ensuring sustainable growth. Adopting AI technologies involves not only integrating advanced tools and systems but also transforming organizational culture, processes, and strategies. This section outlines key strategies and steps for preparing your organization for an AI-driven future, focusing on organizational readiness, strategic alignment, and practical implementation.

1. Developing a Strategic Vision for AI

A clear and strategic vision for AI is essential for guiding its implementation and integration:

- **Define Objectives**: Start by identifying the key objectives and goals you aim to achieve with AI. Whether it's enhancing operational efficiency, improving customer experiences, or driving innovation, having a well-defined purpose will help align AI initiatives with your organization's strategic priorities.

- **Assess Business Needs**: Conduct a thorough assessment of your organization's needs and challenges to determine where AI can have the most impact. This involves evaluating existing processes, identifying areas for improvement, and exploring how AI can address specific pain points or opportunities.

- **Build Leadership Support**: Secure commitment and support from top leadership to drive AI initiatives. Leadership buy-in is crucial for allocating resources, fostering a culture of innovation, and ensuring alignment between AI projects and organizational strategy.

- **Develop a Roadmap**: Create a roadmap for AI adoption that outlines key milestones, timelines, and resource requirements. This roadmap should include short-term and long-term goals, as well as strategies for scaling AI initiatives across the organization.

2. Building a Strong Data Foundation

AI relies on high-quality data to function effectively, making data management a critical component of AI readiness:

- **Data Collection and Integration**: Establish robust data collection processes to gather relevant and accurate data. Integrate data from various sources to create a comprehensive dataset that can be used for AI applications.

- **Data Quality and Governance**: Implement data governance practices to ensure data quality, consistency, and security. This includes data validation, cleaning, and maintenance procedures, as well as compliance with data protection regulations.

- **Data Infrastructure**: Invest in data infrastructure and technologies that support AI initiatives. This may involve upgrading data storage, processing capabilities, and data management systems to handle large volumes of data efficiently.

- **Data Analytics and Tools**: Equip your organization with the necessary tools and technologies for data analysis. This includes data visualization, analytics platforms, and machine learning frameworks that facilitate the development and deployment of AI models.

3. Developing AI Talent and Skills

Building a skilled workforce is essential for successfully implementing and managing AI technologies:

- **Identify Skill Gaps**: Assess the current skills and competencies within your organization to identify gaps related to AI and data science. This will help you determine the specific skills and expertise needed for successful AI integration.

- **Recruit and Train Talent**: Invest in recruiting skilled professionals with expertise in AI, machine learning, and data science. Additionally, provide training and development opportunities for existing employees to build their AI-related skills and knowledge.

- **Foster a Culture of Learning**: Promote a culture of continuous learning and innovation within your organization. Encourage employees to stay updated on AI trends, technologies, and best practices through workshops, seminars, and industry events.

- **Leverage External Expertise**: Consider partnering with external experts, consultants, or academic institutions to gain insights and support for AI initiatives. Collaborating with external partners can provide valuable expertise and accelerate AI adoption.

4. Implementing AI Solutions

Successful implementation of AI solutions requires careful planning and execution:

- **Pilot Projects**: Start with pilot projects to test AI solutions on a smaller scale before full deployment. This allows you to assess the effectiveness of AI applications, identify potential challenges, and make necessary adjustments.

- **Integration with Existing Systems**: Ensure that AI solutions are seamlessly integrated with existing systems and workflows. This involves aligning AI tools with current processes, data sources, and technology infrastructure.

- **Change Management**: Implement change management strategies to facilitate the adoption of AI within your organization. Communicate the benefits of AI, address any concerns or resistance, and provide support to employees as they adapt to new technologies.

- **Monitoring and Evaluation**: Continuously monitor and evaluate the performance of AI solutions to ensure they meet your objectives. Use key performance indicators (KPIs) and metrics to track progress, measure outcomes, and identify areas for improvement.

5. Ensuring Ethical and Responsible AI Use

Ethical considerations are critical for ensuring that AI technologies are used responsibly and align with organizational values:

- **Develop Ethical Guidelines**: Establish ethical guidelines and principles for AI use within your organization. This includes ensuring fairness, transparency, and accountability in AI decision-making processes.

- **Address Bias and Fairness**: Implement measures to detect and address biases in AI models and applications. Conduct regular audits and assessments to ensure that AI systems operate fairly and do not perpetuate discrimination.

- **Ensure Data Privacy and Security**: Protect personal and sensitive data by implementing robust data privacy and security measures. Comply with relevant regulations and industry standards to safeguard data and maintain user trust.

- **Promote Human Oversight**: Ensure that AI systems are subject to human oversight and intervention, particularly in critical decision-making scenarios. This helps prevent overreliance on AI and ensures that ethical considerations are taken into account.

6. Fostering Innovation and Collaboration

Encouraging innovation and collaboration can drive the successful integration of AI:

- **Encourage Innovation**: Create an environment that fosters innovation and experimentation with AI. Support initiatives that explore new AI applications, technologies, and business models.
- **Promote Collaboration**: Encourage collaboration between different departments, teams, and external partners to leverage diverse perspectives and expertise. Collaborative efforts can lead to more effective AI solutions and drive organizational growth.
- **Stay Updated on Trends**: Keep abreast of emerging AI trends, technologies, and industry developments. Staying informed about the latest advancements can help you identify new opportunities and adapt to changes in the AI landscape.

Preparing your organization for an AI-driven future involves developing a strategic vision, building a strong data foundation, investing in talent and skills, implementing AI solutions effectively, ensuring ethical use, and fostering innovation. By taking these steps, organizations can navigate the complexities of AI adoption, leverage its potential benefits, and position themselves for long-term success in an increasingly AI-driven world. Embracing AI with a strategic and responsible approach will enable organizations to enhance their operations, drive innovation, and achieve sustainable growth.

www.ingramcontent.com/pod-product-compliance
Lightning Source LLC
LaVergne TN
LVHW051441050326
832903LV00030BD/3192